John Bainbridge is the author of over thirty books about the British countryside and walking, as well as historical and mystery novels. He has been a rambler and hillwalker for over fifty years, and has been commended by the Ramblers Association for his many years of voluntary work in the rambling movement. John spent nine years as chief executive of the Dartmoor Preservation Association .

Non-Fiction
The Compleat Trespasser
Rambling – The Beginner's Bible
Footloose With George Borrow
Easy British Bakes and Cakes

Fiction
Balmoral Kill
The Shadow of William Quest
Loxley
A Seaside Mourning
A Christmas Malice
The Seafront Corpse

Further Information:

Walking writer John Bainbridge has a regular rambling and access blog at www.thefreedomtoroam.com

First Published as a paperback by Fellside Books in 2016

ISBN-13: 978-1519736406 ISBN- 10: 1519736401

WAYFARER'S DOLE

Rambles in the British Countryside

In medieval times pilgrims travelling the road through Winchester to Canterbury would halt at the St Cross Hospital, a place of rest and refuge for those on holy journeys, and demand the Wayfarer's Dole - small portions of ale and bread to ease the hunger and thirst incurred on their travels.

By John Bainbridge
Author of "The Compleat Trespasser"

Fellside Books

She is not any common Earth
Water or wood or air,
But Merlin's Isle of Gramarye,
Where you and I will fare.
          Puck's Song, Rudyard Kipling

Wayfarer's Dole

Beginnings

A stormy dawn on Dartmoor and I was mightily glad of the huge granite boulder that protected me from the worst of the rain. The rocky heights of Laughter Tor loom out of the mist, causing me to crawl even deeper into my sleeping bag, reflecting on the momentary madness that inspired me to seek shelter on the exposed summit of Bellever.

I should have brought a tent, instead of this flimsy waterproof flapping in the wind. I don't often use a tent. The true tramper sleeps out in fine weather and seeks cover in the wet. But no tramper in his right mind would ever seek shelter on top of a storm-blown tor. There have been some strange bedrooms on my tramps around Britain, but few as wet and cold as Bellever in April.

I'd tramped across northern Dartmoor the day before, rain-lashed most of the way, not seeing a soul. I'd watched the clouds break across the highest summits in southern England, and heard the curlew's cry echo across the peat-bogs of Cranmere and Cut Hill.

On that solitary ramble I had the feeling, familiar to all who wander in wild places, that I was the only human left in the world.

The rain cleared as I strode the last few miles along the Dart river, its white water forcing through rocky channels and tearing at grass and moss on its banks. Then I saw the rocky crown of Bellever in the distance, the tor that stands high and proud at the very heart of the moor, visible for miles from all directions. Where better to sleep on a long Dartmoor tramp?

A clear sky gave me an hour or two to sit on the very top of the rocky hill, to reflect on my journey there, a long walk from one end of Dartmoor to another. I'd wandered the British countryside since childhood and had come to know Dartmoor well.

The route I took from Okehampton to Ivybridge would be thirty-one miles in all, across some of the loneliest country in the land. In years to come I would do the walk in a day, but then I broke my travels in half, Bellever being the midpoint of a glorious exploration.

I was sixteen, rootless, dreading endless years of wage slavery. That day I'd negotiated rock-clittered hillsides, lonely river valleys and acres of mire and bog. I'd not seen a soul all day, and I was content. I wanted more of this. More solitude, more freedom, more joy, a sense of relationship with the great walkers of the past, read about in the considerable literature of rambling, who walked, like ghosts, through my life.

I crawled into a niche between the rocks and settled down to sleep, thinking of those walkers who had come before, a great vision of vagrom men and women – the pilgrims, the literary tramps, the gentle ramblers, the brave souls who had fought for access to our countryside. As I looked up at the stars, I made a vow to devote my life to exploring my country on foot, writing my own account of my travels, trespassing across denied landscapes, skirmishing for the freedom to roam, fighting for my own liberty.

I would walk, mostly, alone, but would seek the company of rambling friends so that I might share their greater knowledge of people and places. I had been a wanderer since childhood and would make the wandering life my personal mission, walking the wild places of Britain until the last breath.

I descended from Bellever on that rainy dawn, with my whole life mapped out. I felt peace of mind, something only ever achieved during rambles in those youthful days. The descent from the heart of the moor was the beginning of my journey.

~

Forty years later: I stood on a summit far distant from Dartmoor, thinking of that night on Bellever. Like most youthful dreams, mine had been compromised. I had not always been free to walk – but I'd experienced more free days than most people held captive by the lure of so-called civilisation.

I had led the outdoor life a lot of the time; unhappy when I had sold out working for others inside the dungeon confines of the workaday world. But even then I had days of freedom. Closing my eyes I can picture a thousand hills, hundreds of trails, feel the lash of the rain and wind, the cry of rivers. All in the memory where old walks dwell. I had succeeded better than most in fulfilling that early dream.

I had come to know many walkers, though few dedicated to my life of vagabondage. They had mostly understood my needs, sympathising with my ambitions. I could see their faces as I sat on that hilltop. Good friends, their companionship still cherished, though I only sought them out as a change from solitary roaming.

Most have gone. As you grow old, you walk more with the ghosts of fellow wanderers, summoned by memory. Dead they may be, but I carry their experiences and knowledge on every walk. In different ways they all helped me to find my feet.

The mountain summit was Silver How, in England's Lake District. All around were hills known from long days on high ridges. The Lakes stretched away from me like so many mirrors reflecting the blue of the sky. Juniper filled the gullies cutting into the mountain slopes.

A good clear summer's day; every rock, tree and drystone wall sharply delineated by the sun. Far below a tiny boat broke the stillness of Grasmere's silver waters. A gentle breeze stirred the Herdwick sheep gathered amidst the rocks. All seemed quiet. I sat against a boulder in the shelter of the hill, and felt at peace.

My favourite hill is the one I'm on. But the views from mountains such as Silver How are a reminder that there are far too many mountains to scale in one lifetime. Climbing every summit in the Lake District is achievable, but in places like Scotland, where you look out on hundreds of mountain tops, you realise the shortness and fragility of human life. You settle for doing your best, seeing over as many horizons as possible.

Despite a lifetime of roaming I have achieved little. Delightful corners of the British Isles remain unvisited. I mourn for all the places I shall never see, whether they be the highest tops or the quiet meadows crossed by untasted country footpaths.

The British are lucky, though many take the beauty of their land for granted. In very little space we have mountains and downlands, marshlands and deep woods, all crying out to be explored. In our overcrowded land it is still possible to spend hours and even days away from other people. To hear the haunting cry of the curlew rather than incessant human chatter, to lie on a hilltop and scan unbroken vistas of green countryside. These delights may not last for ever, for our land is always under threat. But while it is there we should all enjoy it, and fight to protect it, lest accounts such as this become an epitaph for something irretrievably lost.

Is there a better way to explore our countryside than on foot? Walking is now the most popular pastime in Britain. The great outdoors is calling and many are answering that heart cry on at least an occasional basis, on a guided ramble perhaps, a day out with a walking club, or a rural stroll. Days out in the midst of busy lives.

But there are other individuals, those whom I call vagabond men and women who live to walk, yearning to know the scene over the hill, never happy unless they are roaming through Britain's wild and lonely places.

I remember a day in Scotland, standing on a footbridge by the waterfalls in Glen Orchy. I had had a long journey without seeing a soul, when three motorcyclists pulled in from the narrow lane through the glen. One of them, wiry and red-headed, turned to me explaining how they worked in Edinburgh, motor biking through the Highlands most weekends for the feeling of space it gave them. He looked with longing up the track leading into the mountains and told me what he *really* wanted to do was to take to the hills for weeks on end, with just a pack on his back. I nodded in agreement for I know that feeling. Such are the desires of the outdoor man or woman who never feels at ease until such needs are satisfied, and then wants more and more.

Those of us who enjoy exploring Britain on foot follow in an honourable tradition. In medieval times pilgrims travelling the road through Winchester to Canterbury would halt at the St Cross Hospital, a place of rest and refuge for those on holy journeys, and demand the Wayfarer's Dole - small portions of ale and bread to ease the hunger and thirst incurred on their travels. Even now, when pilgrimages are few and far between, you may stop at St Cross and receive this ancient refreshment in a delightful echo of past days, a wonderful link with ancient times.

We are all pilgrims in our way and there is a point to most journeys on foot. Despite our crowded cities and car-choked roads, we live in one of the most beautiful countries on earth. For sheer variety of scenery the British Isles are unbeatable. From the snow-capped mountains of Scotland to the lonely Pennines, from the marshlands of the Fens to the rugged moors and coastline of the West Country we have a land that demands to be explored. The best way to see it is on foot.

And every step we take is a stride into our own history. The ridge paths of southern England were used at least as far back as the Iron Age, centuries old when Alfred the Great and his Saxon armies marched their long horizons. That footpath across a field might be the remnants of a Roman road or an ancient drovers' route. Wayside shrines remain to show us where pilgrims halted. There are traces of narrow ways down to lonely coves, once used by the pack-ponies of smugglers, there to be enjoyed by the coastal walker.

The people of Britain have always walked, either on pilgrimages or for their work, but walking for pleasure is relatively new. In not very distant days those travelling on foot in Britain without a reasonable purpose might well be labelled 'rogues and vagabonds', and were often treated as eccentric or downright dangerous. The Swiss traveller Carl Philip Moritz, who walked from London to the Peak District in 1782, remarked that:

a traveller on foot in this country seems to be considered as a sort of wild man or an out-of-the-way being who is stared at, pitied, suspected, and shunned by everybody that meets him…in England any person undertaking so long a journey on foot is sure to be looked upon and considered as either a beggar, or a vagabond, or some necessitous wretch, which is a character not much more popular than a rogue.

And much of Moritz's journey was on roads. He seldom ventured into a surrounding countryside that was mostly unenclosed. From medieval times workers had been expected to remain and to labour within their own localities, though some of the better off could seek sanction to travel as pilgrims. The Victorian rural chronicler Richard Jefferies tells of seeing a notice giving the stark warning:

All persons found wandering abroad, lying, lodging, or being in any barn, outhouse, or in the open air, and not giving a good account of themselves, will be apprehended as rogues and vagabonds, and be either publicly whipt or sent to the house of correction, and afterwards disposed of according to law, by order of the magistrates. Any person who shall apprehend any rogue or vagabond will be entitled to a reward of ten shillings.

But even by Richard Jefferies's time the middle classes, enthused by the romantic legacy of poets such as William Wordsworth, had invented the concept of the walking tour, exploring the grandeurs of their own land rather than the wonders of Greece or Italy. It took a further century before the working classes were given the passport to walk for pleasure and leisure. In the more egalitarian years of the twentieth century, rambling clubs thrived, national parks and long distance trails were created, and footpaths and bridleways marked on Ordnance Survey maps.

I suppose I have always had this need for vagabondage. I was brought up in Staffordshire in the remnants of what had once been considerable countryside, interrupted now and again by the relics of the Industrial Revolution. Not far away, within walking distance, was the Black Country - in those days an extensive manufacturing district where the smog would linger in the air for days on end, giving the clouds a colouring as grey as iron.

Though born in a hospital that had once been part of the workhouse of one of the Black Country towns, I was soon transported to what was essentially an idyllic rural landscape. I was scarcely crawling before I attempted to seek out the fields behind the house, always to be dragged back. As I grew into childhood I explored further and further, always happier to be out of the house than in. I suppose even then there was not much actual countryside left, but it seemed a wilderness to me and never failed to tempt me out into a wonder land of hedgerows, wide fields and rough ground.

Quite regularly, tramps would knock the door to ask for hot water for a drum up of tea. I found these strange wanderers mysterious, and envied them as they set out on a journey into the land beyond the distant horizon.

The immediate geography of a child is fixed and it is human nature to push out those boundaries. As I grew older I walked further and further discovering the secrets of every hedgerow, the size and crops of each field. A river ran not far from the house and I followed its banks for many miles. I had an uncle. Not a real uncle but a former neighbour of my grandparents. He had the lust for exploration. Each Sunday he would call for me and we would go off together on longer walks. There were no hills or mountains such as the ones I read about so avidly, but there were the giant slag heaps of abandoned mines, steep and ash-grey, smoking out obnoxious gases like angry volcanoes.

He introduced me to the land beyond the canal, the boundary of my early travels. A stranger land than ours, countryside but with more industry. Narrow boats still worked the Cut trailing butties full of coal. He knew many of the boatmen and would get us lifts on our journeys. He was a collector of people and we would stop to talk to every passing tramp and were welcomed into the encampments where the last Black Country Romanies clung on to an existence. I envied these people their wilder lifestyle and longed to join them.

Sometimes we would journey out to places like Kinver, where it was possible to walk on rock, seek modest precipices and scramble up cliffs. This was my first taste of wilder countryside. It made the fields nearer to home seem very tame. Longer expeditions took me to the hills and vales of the Peak District, my first taste of higher summits. Then childhood holidays brought me to Dartmoor, the first great area of wilderness that I came to know really well.

These early experiences fed my desire for exploration, showing me the sheer variety of landscape in my native land. Mountains and lowlands, forests and marsh, all there to be discovered and added to the memory.

In the course of my adventures I sampled the best that Britain has to offer from the crags of Scotland to the flatlands of East Anglia, from the downlands and hangers of the south country to the rugged moors of the north. I walked in all weathers too. You cannot get a feel of the real Britain unless you have been rain-lashed on its moors, navigated mountains in the thickest cloud, or tramped the Downs on hot sunny days, when all is clear and the blue of the English Channel glimmers in the distance.

I became fascinated with the way walking routes developed through time, took delight in the tiny parish churches where pilgrims left the mark of crosses carved near the porch door, recognised the influence of old manor houses on their local parishes and observed how forgotten industries shaped the land.

I met interesting people too, landowners and farmers, tramps and Romanies, adventurers and those with a rich enthusiasm for their own neighbourhoods. In my travels I encountered mostly the best, and just occasionally the worst, of the British people.

As someone who loves books it has been a great pleasure to seek out the literature of walking, of which there is a great deal, for the wandering life has inspired some of our finest writers. What better on housebound days than to read about the outdoors, using books as an inspiration for walking expeditions. Everywhere I go in these islands I think of writers who have trod the same roads and pathways.

I've remained an inveterate trespasser, believing that the land is the common heritage of us all. Our countryside should be accessible without unreasonable restrictions. I've walked where I like, but always with reverence and care. I need the countryside and walking for me is not just the outward experience of exploration, but an inward journey into the mind that perceives the joyful scene all around.

Resting on the summit of Silver How, I reflected on the long lifetime of walks that had brought me there on that peaceful day. I looked across to the greater summits of Fairfield and Wetherlam, Seat Sandal and the Langdale Pikes, familiar old friends, scenes of so many adventures and memories.

Many of my contemporaries had devoted their lives to seeking out wealthy lifestyles and fulfilling suburban ambitions. I only ever wanted the freedom to keep roaming. As I made the descent from mountain summit to lakeshore, I thought back on my travels - the climbs, the long tramps along ancient tracks, the trespassing through forbidden woodlands.

The excursions of a wanderer.

I walked on.

Over the Stile

Boxing booths were quite a feature of fairs in my youth, usually just a makeshift ring in the open air or inside a tent, where the resident champion would take on all comers from the local population. The champion fighter I encountered in one was a hard physical specimen, with a tough, stubbled face and challenging eyes as dark as his thick black hair.

We wandered across the field to the inn on the old turnpike road, the fairground crowds parting to let the champion through. As we walked I asked how he had got into boxing?

He told me that he had been born near Dudley and came from an old fighting family. "I worked on the canals a bit when I were a lad, then did some coalmining. It were a tough place we lived. You learned to use your fists. I were down the mines five years and that were enough. I started to cough badly, and then one day I coughed up some blood and felt as weak as water. That was enough for me. I dey go in to work that day, nor any other."

"It must have been frightening?"

"Frightening wor in it! I thought I wor on me way out, pal. My mining days were up. I certainly wor gonna die to make some other bugger rich!"

"So what did you do next?" I asked, as we sat over two pints of ale in a corner of the old pub.

"Hung about on the dole for a couple of years. Did some thieving. Only from big business, mind. I had scruples of a sort. Then one day this bloke come looking round the family for someone who might do a bit of bare knuckle fighting. Illegal and all that, but the money was good. I kept it up for a while, made a pile, then started boxing with the gloves on. One week the fair came to town and I left with it. Always wanted to roam a bit!"

"In the boxing booth?"

"Not at first, no. Worked on the rides. Then one day the chap in the boxing booth got knocked down by a local, then again the next day, then the next…lost his bottle, I suppose. So I took over and I've been at it ever since. Not that it'll be for much longer. The fairs are goin' and the boxing booths are goin' faster. I doubt yoh'l see one ten years from now. All the colour's goin' from England."

I nodded in agreement, for so it seemed to me.

"You'll go back to the Midlands?"

"Mebbe, though that's all changed since my time there." He glanced sideways at me. "Yoh'm from the Black Country, ay yer?"

"I was born there, but I haven't really been back since I was a boy."

"I thought so. It's there, in the voice. Yoh cor lose it altogether."

~

I've thought often of him over the years, and wondered what became of him. I remember too the Midlands of my childhood. Although I was born in a Black Country town, I was brought up in what was then a considerable stretch of countryside at Great Barr, a few miles out of West Bromwich. It was across the fields thereabouts that I first began to walk.

We lived in a house situated on was still a country lane, winding round in its later stages to cross a railway line and then the brown waters of the River Tame. Some way along the lane was an old wartime ammunition dump, a marvellous and deserted playground of old huts and bunkers, where an adventurous child could disappear for much of a long summer day.

Footpaths led across fields that could not have changed much in centuries. I recall them most at harvest time, when sometimes we would help the farmer gather in the crops until well after dusk. The fields around were a source of challenge and adventure, leading up to the raised embankment of the canal, the first boundary to be negotiated in childhood explorations.

Years later I acquired an old map showing the district in Victorian times, when it was a vast stretch of countryside, the towns of the Black Country mere extended settlements, not much more than large villages in a setting still essentially rural. When I came to read the novels of D. H. Lawrence I could well understand their settings, that heady mixture of industrial and bucolic.

On reflection I had rather a Lawrencian upbringing, for my first school was in the mining village of Hamstead, its buildings right next door to a busy colliery. Many of the pupils were the children of miners, and the great coal buckets passed overhead along thick wires strung between gantries, coal dust blowing down over the school yard.

Our headmaster, a fierce man, but not unkind, would tell us that if we didn't work hard at school we would end up working much, much harder down the mine.

As I walked home I would reflect on that, yet within a mile or so I had left all of that industry behind and was out in the fields again. Sometimes, I would see the miners on my walks, for they loved to ramble and many had a fine knowledge of natural history. Such a background would have been so familiar to my boxing opponent. In later life I got the chance to go down a working coal mine. I knew that I wouldn't have lasted a day at such hard labour. My admiration for coal miners is boundless.

I wandered freely across this land, as indeed we all did, for the concepts of trespass and public rights of way were unknown to us. I suspect that it was this early conditioning that turned me into the inveterate trespasser of later years for, to quote Sir Leslie Stephen, I have no 'superstitious reverence' for absolute rights to property.

I grew up in a freer world, perhaps, and the country landowners of this childhood landscape would have had to turn many a blind eye to roaming locals, some as ferocious and tough as the fairground boxer from near Dudley.

Perhaps my favourite childhood walk was across the fields to the canal. The path took off from the bend in the country lane, a broad track at first leading to a near derelict barn and the ruins of a house. I had no idea when the place had fallen into disrepair, but I found its remnants fascinating, seeking out the broken shards of pottery that might be found amid the rubble, and tearing away the several layers of wallpaper that still clung to the tumbling walls. There were bats somewhere in the ruin, and at evening time barn owls hunted over the neighbouring meadows. I scared others with tales of ghosts, of former inhabitants who wailed at the dismal spectacle that had once been their home.

My friends believed my stories and certainly, returning that way in the dark, I half-believed them myself. A path led across the fields and in a very little while I seemed to be way out in the countryside, though I suspect the bounds of the territory were much smaller than I have remembered. Not much of a walk brought me to the great embankment, along the top of which ran the canal. I would amble along the towpaths for many miles. In those days there were still narrow boats working its waters, though they were becoming few and far between.

Of great interest to me were the high bridges, where the navigators had placed the canal over the river and railway. Traversing the brickwork of these over what seemed to be dizzying heights were a great challenge and I was a fearless climber in the days before I learned discretion.

But what I remember most of all was the silence. This landscape might be at the heart of the industrial Midlands, but it was quiet and peaceful. It was that I loved best. It was something to look forward to, at weekends or on days when I bunked off school, my drink and 'piece' in an old army knapsack and the thrill of miles of lonely walking ahead. Those boyhood peregrinations set the theme for the rest of my roaming life.

But those quiet lands are no more. One day, not long ago, driving back from the Lake District, I decided to see if I could recapture something of the magic of those past days. I parked the car outside my childhood home and walked once more down the lane. At first the prospects seemed good, the fields opposite the house leading down to the river had survived, offering grazing for horses as they always had. But at the bend in the lane I was met with an awful sight.

The old ammunition dump had vanished completely. In its place, high overhead on huge concrete piers was the motorway, tearing above the fields and over the canal where I had so often rambled, with no sympathy whatsoever for the land beneath, which was now squashed and tamed in its hideous shadow.

What had once been an oasis of peace was now noise stained with the heavy rumble of cars and lorries. As if to add insult to this injury, a footpath sign indicated a track running parallel with the motorway, inviting me to follow along a section of the 'Tame Way'.

But, I thought, who would want to? At least along this section where the once charming remnants of rural south Staffordshire had been sacrificed for society's mania for speed and hurry.

I cursed the unimaginative bastards who had desecrated the country of my childhood. I hope that there is some suitable and very hot place awaiting them in the furnaces of hell, preferably a corner where their hearing is constantly assaulted by the rush of motor traffic.

I remembered the warning of the Black Country boxer that it had all changed. He was right. It was changed almost beyond recognition.

Perhaps we should never go back.

~

The other day, thinking back on my many rambles, I remembered the time I deserted from the staid world of responsibility and took to the roads. The occasion marked an important stage along the pathways into roaming and vagabondage.

I was sixteen when I walked out of my home in Teignmouth to do the usual train journey to the technical college in Torquay, where I was studying – not from choice – retailing and business studies. I say studying… in fact I did very little work, dreaming away at the back of the class, more interested in surreptitiously reading novels than trying to understand the finer points of a balance sheet. Mind, I still passed the exams. God knows how!

Where was I?

Ah, yes, I was walking down to the railway station on my way to another eight hours of captivity. But it was a beautiful day, the sun was shining, the sky was blue…

If it had been the weekend I'd be going out for a walk. Probably Dartmoor, certainly somewhere deep in the countryside. Trying to forget that the spectre of Monday morning is always there to haunt you the moment you break free on Friday. Worse for people these days who often have to work at the weekends as well.

I didn't consciously turn left away from the railway station. I really didn't. I can't think now how I came to be walking along the sea wall towards Dawlish. But I can remember the incredible feeling of freedom that surged through my mind.

The sea lapped gently against the wall and the red sandstone cliffs beyond. I remember being reminded of long childhood holidays when I roamed where I liked and liberty was my watchword. I sat on a bench and spent an hour watching the ships heading up the English Channel.

It seemed a hell of a good way to spend the time. If I thought for a moment about what I was supposed to be doing – the train journey having the same old conversations, signing the register at the college to prove I was there, looking at a blackboard and trying to grasp the principles of double-entry book-keeping – well, I don't remember thinking about any of that at all.

I walked on into Dawlish and spent a few very pleasant hours reading a novel in one of the shelters by the Dawlish Water. The book was Bram Stoker's *Dracula* by the way. Fun doing that instead of commercial arithmetic. I went up to the baker's shop and got some bread and fed the ducks. It was all very pleasant.

Then, after this lovely interval, I walked on, up the lane past Luscombe Castle with its woods crowding in from both sides.

The birds sang. Pheasants scampered across the road. I was on very familiar ground – I'd regularly trespassed on this private estate, found the secret paths in the greenwood, dodged the keepers. Wondered why it was private anyway.

It's a steep climb, up that lane – for Little Haldon Moor which stands at the top is eight hundred feet above sea level. It was an area I knew well. I'd explored every inch of it in the days before I could easily get to Dartmoor. Made camp-fires in the little disused quarry at the head of Smallacombe Goyle, walked the ramparts of the Iron Age hill fort close to Ashcombe Tower. Tried to find the battlefield where Athelstan, the Saxon King, defeated King Huwel of the Cornish a thousand years before. Looked for the secret well at Lidwell Chapel, which was supposedly haunted by the ghost of a mad monk.

Now a gentle breeze swept east from the blue fringe of the Dartmoor hills. I walked across the hillside and into the trees, down towards the paths and lanes leading down to the Teign estuary.

Forty years later I devised a long walk around this area – the Teignmouth and Dawlish Way – you can buy a booklet from the local rambling group and follow in my footsteps. Despite the over-development of much of this part of Devon, my route takes you through some wild places – little changed since that day I bunked off college and roamed these hillsides.

And it was somewhere about there that I discovered a kind of spiritual freedom that I was to know for the first time. A feeling that I was as much a part of the landscape as the gorse that clustered to the edge of the hill-ridges, the heather that covered the moorland and the wind that stirred the boughs of the trees. The knowledge that I was wandering not just through a landscape but *in* the landscape. Not really a physical experience as much as something indefinable within the mind and the soul.

The feeling was addictive and as I walked down to the river I made up my mind to do the walk again the next day and the next. And so I did, roaming further each time. Not new countryside to me, for I'd walked it all many times, but now I felt that I was really seeing it, as though my eyes were opened. They were a hot few days so I lingered in the more delightful spots. Lay back in the heather and gazed up into the blue of the sky for immeasurable periods of time, seeming to float somewhere between the physicality of the earth and existence and something else. It was I believe my first experience of summit fever.

It couldn't last of course. The college missed me and reported my absence. I felt a kind of duty to my family to see the course through, to at least pass the examinations. So the dungeon doors clanged shut. The escape route out of captivity was discovered. But it was not to last long.

During the wet summer of 1974, I was perambulating the boundary of the Forest Of Dartmoor with rambling friends. We were crossing the route of the old tramway that once brought china clay down from Redlake. Wild hills all around, moorland seemingly beyond measure. The rain had stopped for an hour and the breeze had stilled. There is a quietude about Dartmoor in such moments.

It was a rare few hours of freedom. I'd sold out to wage slavery, working very long hours five and often six days of the week. My writing had come almost to a dead halt, bar the occasional magazine article. I was too tired to think of anything much beyond the daily grind.

But that day, as I looked up the hillside towards Three Barrows, I had the flash of an idea, an epiphany that once more flashed the freedom of those Little Haldon days before my mind.

I would quit the job. Write and write and write about my experiences. Lead walks on Dartmoor as a guide to supplement my income. And then explore all of those places that were just names on a map. I mightn't make much money but I wouldn't be a wage slave either.

And so I did.

There were times when I had to compromise. There were roads I journeyed along which might have been better avoided. But the hills and woods were too tempting to ignore.

No Man's Land

On a flinty track high above the headwaters of a Devon river I met a Romany, his wagon hauled close in beneath a tree, the blue smoke of his fire drifting lazily into the forest. He smiled, waving a greeting as I approached. He offered me tea. We sat together on a fallen log and he mourned for the wayfaring life he had known as a boy.

"It wasn't easy, 'specially in this south country. The gavvers would wait till you'd set up camp and then shift you. If you lasted a day or two you did well. In those days families were quite territorial, there was none of this wandering up and down the country - though we'd go further for the horse fairs."

"Do you stay in the West Country now?"

"Well, I'm on my own now, so I come and go as I please. I gets a bit of casual work, clearing timber or maybe helping out on farms, hedging and ditching. But I travel all over. A few months ago I was in Norfolk, where I've family. But I prefer the north. More places to pull in, you see."

I sipped my tea from a battered old mug. "Are people more welcoming these days?"

"No, not really. Countryside's full of townies who've bought up all the cottages or had bungalows built. They have their piece of heaven. Heaven forbid if anyone wants to share it with them. Most of my people can't take it anymore and have become house-dwellers."

"You've never thought of that?"

"No. I was born to roam and roam I will till the day I drop. Couldn't imagine not being able to move on."

"Where will you go next?"

"Got the promise of a bit of work over to Dorset. Place I pitch close to Dorsetshire Gap. Know it?"

Yes, I knew it. Dorsetshire Gap. That strange junction of ancient paths hidden away in one of the county's most secretive stretches of countryside. A little piece of old England, seldom visited except by those in the know. A mystical place for meetings. Old when Saxon armies rallied there. Dorsetshire Gap. A portion of this realm that seems to have escaped the feel and betrayal of recent centuries. I'd met Gypsies there. I told the old man of some of my encounters, and how I had made camp there and lived for a while the vagabond life.

"There are some places you hold in special regard," he nodded. "You see the barrows round there? All them dead people of thousands of years ago who all walked the tracks we take. How dare they say we have no right to use the countryside!" he thundered. "We know backwards the places they can't even imagine!"

I have thought often of that old man over the years, but I never saw him again. The Romany race has all but disappeared from the land now, subjected to appalling persecution. Gypsy people either driven off the roads or herded into mean reservations; miniature concentration camps, often in unappealing locations, lest they offend the sensibilities of suburban man. I grew up seeing the remnants of these travelling people on our roads, now a rare sight in this new century except around the times of the horse fairs in the north.

Except in the wildest places, the countryside is not friendly to itinerant wanderers who wish to set up camp. The great tracts of rough ground, the areas of no man's land that once lined so many of our highways, have been grubbed out by road engineers, or fenced off by greedy landowners.

No man's land.

We think of those evocative words now in terms of the disputed territory of a battlefield, perhaps the killing ground between the trenches in the Great War. But they originated describing the acres of English countryside that were literally held by no man. On such stretches of unclaimed land, by the roadside perhaps or on the edge of a common or forest, the forebears of that Gypsy found shelter in a landscape that was gloriously unfettered.

Lowland Britain today is scarcer of such welcoming places; fences and barbed wire channel walkers into increasingly narrow avenues of exploration. Unauthorised camping by the wayside is severely discouraged.

If you seek a symbol for much of lowland Britain, then picture a strand of barbed wire.

But the long ridges to the east of Devon are generally free to roam; Woodbury Common, Mutters Moor, Fire Beacon, West Hill Strips, and Harcombe Hill. Such lovely names. High ground, much of it. Important lowland heaths of heather and gorse, the home of the nightjar on summer evenings. A place where birds of prey whirl and hover over stretches of broadleaved woodland. It was by the trees of one of the ridges that I met that wise old Gypsy. Such encounters are few and far between, for it is rare to even encounter another walker in the lonely forests away from the more popular commons.

The path from Sidford leading to Knowle House, a lovely old manor house, is now tarmaced, but still attractive as it winds uphill from the River Sid, alongside the Snod Brook. I have walked this way so many times and at all seasons of the year, though it is best in springtime when the slopes of the hills are filled with bluebells.

Sidford's main street still boasts some pretty cottages, a number of them thatched, though its outskirts have been wrecked by urban sprawl. Its ruination is soon left behind as you enter the rural tranquillity that surrounds the Snod Brook and the picturesque hamlet of Harcombe. The hills beyond Harcombe are a kind of wild frontier; the place where the over-developed south coastline of Devon ends and a quieter pastoral land begins. It is a steep ascent, a kind of testing ground of your determination to find the peace that lies beyond. Breathless you arrive at the top and leave the surfaced road behind and head out into the woodland up a rough and muddy track.

On the edge of Harcombe Hill is a viewpoint over Sidmouth, with the great sandstone bulge of High Peak, swelling out of the line of the coast. I know that hill well. Its summit, though, is usually missed by the thousands of walkers travelling the South West Coast National Trail, who all go inland around its substantial flanks.

Hidden on its top are the remains of a causewayed enclosure, each year tumbling a little more into the sea. Causewayed enclosures probably represent the first attempts, in the Bronze Age, to fence off portions of the English landscape. What they were used for is still unclear; they may well have been tribal gathering places, markets, or centres for ritual. A number exist across southern Britain, though few are visible. High Peak would have been evident from Harcombe Hill, as it is to this day. It is very likely that the people of the Bronze Age walked the very ridge paths that I had come to know so well.

I reflected on this mania for enclosure as I headed through the woodlands towards the higher ground of Harcombe.

How different the world might have been if the land had been shared from the beginning. If outraged early dwellers in our countryside had torn down the banks and fences of their enclosing neighbour, and territorialism had failed.

But it wasn't like that and the evidence is everywhere in lowland Britain. The look of the southern countryside was created by enclosure; from prehistory to modern times, every bank, fence, field, part of the palimpsest which tells the story of our enclosing history.

Much of Harcombe Hill is wooded with ubiquitous conifers outnumbering deciduous trees but, thankfully, its owners have an imaginative programme of restoring the broadleaved woodlands, as the pines mature and are felled. A flavour of the ancient landscape remains, for the ridge way is lined with older trees, oak, ash, beech and holly.

This flinty track keeps to the high ground, climbing ever so gently until it reaches a junction of equally old paths. Not far away is Blackbury Camp, a hill fort from the Iron Age, perhaps a descendant in design and purpose of the older causewayed enclosures. I wandered down to it and found its great banks and ditches hidden quite charmingly between tall trees. A glance at the map shows that many of the lanes and footpaths used today are probably at least as old as the hill fort, if not more ancient.

Returning to my original walking route, I followed a ridge path up to Broad Down. This was once a great stretch of open countryside, but its considerable acreage is now fenced and presents a forbidden look, despite being mapped as open countryside under access legislation. Broad Down is Devon's largest Bronze Age necropolis outside Dartmoor. Despite its encircling fences it still boasts an untamed feeling, as though it is something apart from the ploughed and grazed fields around.

There is no doubt that early man held this land to be sacred; a place to bring the dead for the start of their final journey, a site of magic and ritual. As I stood by the wire fence looking across its hallowed acres, I recalled the thundering words of the Gypsy: *All them dead people of thousands of years who all walked the tracks we take. How dare they say we have no right to use the countryside!*

Passing a number of burial mounds, the ridgeway follows the edge of the down and a surfaced lane took me round to Roncombe Goyle. I sat and ate lunch on the edge of the goyle, a deep sandstone cut in the hills.

The tracks around the district have indeed been used for centuries, not least by the smugglers who found these high hidden tracks useful for bringing contraband inland. Roncombe Gate, at the head of the valley, was the scene of a terrible clash between the smugglers and the excise men in November 1787. A local newspaper reported that

...a most inhuman murder was committed on the bodies of William Jenkins and William Scott, late officers in his Majesty's Excise, by a gang of smugglers, when the said officers were in execution of their duty, in attempting to seize some run goods, at a place called Roncombe's Girt, on the road between Honiton and Beer.

Walking these hidden tracks today, it is not difficult to imagine lines of pack-ponies laden with kegs of brandy being led inland from the sea.

The history of England is written across its landscape, but many of its stories are lost unless they were recorded at the time. I once met an old man on the track who had patrolled it looking for enemy parachutists when he was a member of the Home Guard. Little changes. Redcoats once marched up and down these valleys to deter an invasion by Napoleon.

Sometimes, if you sit quietly on the side of an ancient path, you can almost visualise these episodes from history.

~

The view over Roncombe Goyle is one of the best in Devon, a pastoral scene of old meadows and deep valley woodlands, hardly ever visited by tourists. A place of peace, a grazing land for cattle and sheep, with only the cry of a pheasant, the singing of the birds, and the distant barking of a farm dog to break the peace, as you wander down towards the valley of the Sid.

Much of this lovely part of Devon can be explored by walking the East Devon Way, a quiet trail from Exmouth to Lyme Regis which passes through the best of the Devon countryside and some of the most charming of its villages. It was a steep section of that trail that I used to regain the height of the ridge, before following the path as it contoured the hillside above Mincombe Wood, the deep azure glaze of bluebells clouding the forest floor, in numbers beyond imagination. The very best sight of an English spring.

One summer evening, long ago, I watched badgers gambolling in play in the steep fields beyond the wood, the valley echoing with their satisfied grunts. It made me recall the poet Edward Thomas's description of those much persecuted creatures as "that most ancient Briton of English beasts". There are deer in this valley too, though you need to be alone and walk quietly to glimpse them.

Walking back to Sidford by Buckley Wood, I found a smallholding that had two oxen grazing in a field, and a Gypsy bow wagon in its yard, sights that would have been so familiar to earlier travellers on foot. For most of my long day's walking I had not seen a soul, such is the lonesomeness of these tranquil hills and valleys.

Without Britain's admirable network of public rights of way such places would be inaccessible. I am with that old Gypsy. The original lines of our ancient paths should be preserved, not only that we might find access to the heart of our countryside, but so that we might do so in the footsteps of our ancestors. Britain's network of public footpaths and bridleways might be eccentric to the bureaucratic eye, but it does serve a good purpose as a way of accessing the land without trespassing.

We are fortunate that there are so many footpaths and bridleways - the first the domain of walkers only, the latter that of walkers, cyclists and horse riders. These are now marked on the Ordnance Survey maps and on the Definitive Maps of rights of way kept by local authorities. They are, in law, part of the Queen's Highway, just the same as a country lane, urban road or motorway.

But our rights of way network is probably the most undervalued, certainly the most underfunded, recreational resource in Britain, given that it is open to all. These paths offer excitement and adventure, often hidden behind a stile or shooting gate.

In a delightful little essay on footpaths, the Victorian country writer Richard Jefferies entices us in the exploration of these old paths *'always get over a stile' is the one rule that should be borne in mind by those who wish to see the land as it really is - that is to say, never omit to explore a footpath, for never was there a footpath yet which did not pass something of interest.*

How did such a delightful and often quirky network of paths come about? Fortunately these old routes were not designed by bureaucrats, emerging with, at best, the tacit approval of landowners. Paths were forged around our landscape by people, which is why we have ancient ridgeways across the landscape's highest ground, mostly in use for thousands of years. Routes were defined by the need to avoid marsh and dense woodland.

Here are the ways taken by our prehistoric ancestors as they journeyed for trade with neighbouring tribes or to the sea in search of salt. In the centuries that followed, the ridgeways facilitated the movement of armies. In Saxon times Alfred the Great defeated the Danish invaders by his knowledge of paths that were aged even in his time. Drovers moved their animals to market along these wild and lonely drove routes, their fires burning like beacons in the night as they rested at traditional stopping places. To follow a ridgeway, as many walkers and riders do today, is to walk in the very footsteps of British history.

We have paths that follow the sections of Roman roads bypassed by modern roadmenders, green lanes wind through our forests and pastoral landscapes, some sunk deep into hollow ways with the tread of generations of passers-by. In the vicinity of towns and villages might be found the paths along which our rural ancestors travelled to church or local markets. Here are the wider ways that once echoed to the horns of stage coaches in those heady days before motor traffic demanded straighter routes. Such paths are an important part of our social heritage and should never be taken for granted. They are as much a part of Britain's story as our village churches and prehistoric monuments.

Yet there are those who want this quaint and important network sanitised, revised and destroyed. Some landowners remain hostile to these outlets for recreation and access. Landowning organisations persist in seeking to have the rights of way network "rationalised". Council bureaucrats seek to stamp their unimaginative control over the idea of any paths that do not fit into their brief of easily-controlled and inexpensive "recreational routes". Why, they argue, would anyone really want to walk the way that local people went to church, or in the footsteps of medieval pilgrims or cattle drovers? Why not straighten the paths, divert them round the edges of the fields they pass through and steer them away from farming hamlets? Why not close some paths altogether?

And yet our history is writ large in these original path-lines. We should no more alter them than we would destroy any of our other valued antiquities. These paths are our common heritage and we should fight hard to protect them.

Moorland

During a long boyhood summer I lived in a hollow on Great Links Tor, a curiously misshapen rock pile which stands like a ruined castle on the border heights of north-western Dartmoor. From the crack along the summit, which served as bedroom and kitchen, I could think back on the day's ramble and gaze both up and down at the local wildlife. In a similar crack on one of the smaller rocks I could watch the ravens feed. High overhead a pair of buzzards wheeled. I envied them their view of the moorland scene. And then there was the old fox.

He would appear about an hour before dusk, stepping gingerly between the clitter of boulders surrounding the tor, alert for danger. Every few paces he would pause and scent the air, nose and ears searching out food and enemies. His legs appeared rheumaticky, his days of speed were long over, though foxes were never intended to be fast animals; watch them hunt and see how economical they are with their movements.

Satisfying himself that his sanctuary was safe, he would nibble at a few whortleberries, limping up onto a flat slab of granite to take in the last strength of the evening sun. As the sunset vanished he shuffled awkwardly to his feet, taking a few deep breaths and going off in search of food. Every evening the ritual was the same and I would plan my expeditions so that I could be back in plenty of time to see my fox, for my own scent to dissipate, so that it wouldn't alarm him. His body was old and worn but his senses seemed as superb as ever.

To do anything which might frighten him away from his familiar haunt would have been shameful. Great Links was the highest point of his territory as it was mine. He was born the creature of the wild that I was striving so desperately to become.

On my last night I waited for my fox to appear. It was one of those evenings when the sky turned several colours as the sun descended behind the Cornish hills. Not a bird or animal made a sound. Even the breeze in the heather quietened, as though the whole world awaited some great event. High upon the tor I hugged the warm lichened rock, waiting for the fox to appear. He was late and I was impatient. Never before had he kept me waiting so long. My mind worked overtime through a sordid procession of snapshots. The gun. The snare. I felt cold inside as the twilight - the dimpsy they call it on Dartmoor - wrapped itself around the hills and coombes. Sheep bleated as they crept between boulders for the night and a raven croaked. But of the old fox there was no sign.

I lay back in the crack in the rock and gazed starwards, listening for the slightest sound of a pad disturbing the heather. As the moon swung across the sky I jumped up a dozen times scrutinising the pale white landscape, but still he did not come. My rucksack was packed well before dawn and I scrambled down the chimney in the rock which was the only access to my refuge. An alarmed bullock paced backwards at the unexpected sight of me and the ewes began to stir and moan. I stretched and splashed my face in a dew pond before pulling on my pack and striding reluctantly downhill away from the tor.

I saw the fox, under a disused railway viaduct where the moorland met the fields of the in-country. He was caught in a metal cage, a so-called humane trap, the kind of instrument used by the seedier end of the fur market. A bloody mass of feathers at his feet told the whole story. My fox had been enticed into his prison with a dead wood pigeon. Hungry and old, he had not been able to resist such easy food. It had taken but a second for the wire to be tripped and the rusty iron door to crash down behind him.

The fox held me with his eyes as I came closer. Would he remember my scent from around the tor and think me his betrayer? A low growl turned into a pathetic yelp. He seemed to be unhurt. Being old he was perhaps resigned to death, while a younger fox might have damaged himself trying to scrabble a way out. This old character had learned the wisdom of conserving energy and waiting for the better moment. I was determined that he should have his reprieve.

Turning the trap away from myself, I hooked the door with a redundant piece of railway metal and, pulling back, eased it open. My fox breathed deeply for a few seconds before tearing out of the trap. He paused at the far end of the viaduct arch, glancing back for a moment at the trap and at me before slinking into the trees. Heaving the trap onto my shoulders, I headed into the thickest part of the undergrowth and spent a half-hour removing door and trip wire for safety. It was never recovered by its original owners. It was there for a good many years until it rusted away almost completely in the soft Dartmoor rain.

And the fox? I never saw him again in all my trips to Great Links Tor. Perhaps he perished in a long moorland winter, for he was very old.

~

It tends to be the way of the hill-walker that he gets to know one wild area of Britain first, gradually moving out to discover other remote places, often becoming weaned away from the first in the process. Living in Devon it was inevitable that my first point of contact with wilderness was Dartmoor, that much threatened national park.

At first I thought it vast, too much to know in a lifetime but, in reality, compared to wilder areas of Britain, it is small. Sometimes I would walk the length of it in a day, or climb hills and see clear across it. It was the scene of many adventures, conflicts, and days of hard walking. I came to know it well, perhaps too well.

Dartmoor is Britain's most threatened national park, its granite acres occupied and damaged by the military, threatened by quarrying, overgrazed and undergrazed. I spent nine years as chief executive of the Dartmoor Preservation Association (DPA) – one of the oldest environmental pressure groups in Britain – fighting some of those threats. Some we won. Many we lost. I was inspired particularly by Lady Sayer.

Sylvia spent much of the twentieth century fighting so many damaging proposals that would have wrecked Dartmoor. She was for many years the tough uncompromising chairman of the DPA. She took no prisoners. Dartmoor, without her intervention, would have been completely destroyed by now.

Sadly, many who came afterwards in the DPA sold out her legacy, becoming more concerned with preserving the Dartmoor "Establishment" rather than Dartmoor itself. Upholding their own politically loaded views rather than national park values. There are a few exceptions, brave souls who fight on. I salute them and hope that the "Few" will one day triumph. I retired with battle fatigue but, in my mind, I see the best and worst of Dartmoor, the wild and the compromised wild.

~

At first there is absolute stillness, stillness beyond silence, not even the sound of water breaking the peace as it seeps quietly from the great mire into the moorland river. Then skylarks soar into the blue, a curlew cries as the walker becomes accepted as part of the landscape. This is Aune Head in the heart of Dartmoor, the most southerly stretch of lonely country in the British Isles.

In an urbanised and overcrowded southern England it is hard to imagine that there are still such places as this watershed mire - where you can linger for days and see nothing but ground nesting birds, circling buzzards and a scattering of sheep. Walkers are rare and shepherds come just a few times a year to check on their flocks, the calm broken by shouts and the barking of dogs. This part of the moor is a vast plateau with none of the steep slopes and familiar rocky tors of northern Dartmoor. Sometimes the only movements catching the eye are cloud shadows chasing across miles of moor grass, or bog cotton blowing in the breeze. The quarter of a million residents crowded around Plymouth probably don't realise there is such peace and solitude a dozen miles away, though it is waiting for them at the moment when they realise they need to lose the 21st century.

There is no better Dartmoor tramp on a still spring day than to these moorland fastnesses around the long slopes of Ryder, the birthplace of the River Avon, the name the Aune takes as it tumbles a rocky course southwards.

I first discovered Aune Head after ascending Ryder, the highest summit on southern Dartmoor, many years ago. Climbing the hill is the prelude to reaching the secret world of the mire. Ryder is vast, its shoulders and spurs covering a dozen of the wildest square miles of Dartmoor.

Near this line of ascent, twelve knights of King Henry III rode to delineate the bounds of the ancient hunting Forest of Dartmoor from the moorland commons of Devon in 1240. Little has changed in the eight hundred years since. The ground is still as boggy, the moor grass as pale and the views over much of south Devon just as extensive. A sense of space that is rare in southern England.

I have always been fond of this long climb into the wild from Combestone Tor, a strange huddle of rocks atop the deep gorge of the Dart river. It is particularly satisfying. Tramping up Ryder is a bit like being a fly on a gently inclining wall. You feel tiny in the great sweep of the landscape. On harsh winter days with the cold air blowing from the north, your feet crack down on a frozen surface and un-melted hailstones. There is scant shelter on this slope from the unremitting attentions of a fierce gale, except isolated hollows and banks where medieval tinners scratched for tin, or an occasional peat hag. Yet on brighter summer days you can sunbathe on this same hillside, with that feeling that you can reach up and touch the blue of the sky.

Given that Ryder is the highest top on southern Dartmoor, its summit is undramatic. You might hardly know you are there but for an abandoned triangulation post and two older granite stones marking the boundary of Dartmoor Forest. Two great ridges lead off to the cairn-capped subsidiary hills of Snowdon and Huntingdon, and the valley of the Avon. For miles around all is moorland, the great tors of the Dartmoor central belt and the higher summits of the north moor, the great plateau around Cranmere. On sunnier days a patchwork quilt of red and green fields mark the cultivated lands to the south, worn out of old forests by Saxon settlers who would use this moorland for summer grazing.

There is an airy feeling of space. There are no dramatic drops such as you might get in the Lake District or Scotland. Instead the land peels away in great broad swathes, descending so gradually you hardly sense the gradient. Perhaps because of this there is a peculiar sense of connection to the earth, as though you are rooted to the great swelling curve of the Moor. It is interesting that while you may say you are "in" the Lake District or the Peak, you always speak of being "on" Dartmoor.

Certainly this last great wilderness of southern England is not to everyone's taste. Many find it bleak and unappealing and fail to see its subtle beauty. But those who love the Moor, say that the sight of cloud shadows sweeping its heather acres is heart stopping.

A thread of narrow paths leads down from Ryder to Aune Head. Even on summer days these give some indication of how wet the ground is. Boots squelch and sink slightly through the grass and into the peat. Then a wider track, or rather series of roughly parallel pathways, is reached - the Sandy Way, which skirts the head of the mire on its journey from Holne to Princetown.

Two hundred years ago when French and American prisoners of war were incarcerated at Princetown, a market was held just inside the gates so that the captives might buy or barter for food. On market days a colourful procession of local farmers and traders would walk or lead pack ponies along this lonely route to the prison. Now only the occasional rambler follows in their footsteps.

A mile north is a line of crosses, markers on the bare moor, showing an old monastic trail, almost the only man-made objects standing out on the great expanse of heath. Years ago, waylaid by a mist, I discovered their usefulness finding the next before the one behind was quite lost from sight, handholds out of the wilderness. Yet the travellers who took such a route in medieval times would have understood the solitude of traversing wild country in a way that we find difficult to comprehend. Only by being out in the wild for long enough do we cast off the unwelcome comfort of the crowd.

That's why places like Aune Head are not to everyone's taste. One walker I know was overcome with a physical dread at the desolation, the miles of empty moorland, the great mire itself with its pools of water reflecting a grey sky, the bright and weird green of the sphagnum moss and, the utter silence of a winter's day when the birds didn't cry. Dartmoor is like that. You either feel at home in such a place or are overwhelmed and can't wait to get away.

The featurelessness of the moor makes navigation difficult and some walkers have a genuine fear of getting lost. But for those in empathy with these wild surroundings, there are rich rewards, complete peace of mind and a sense of falling out of time, an uncommon feeling on this overcrowded island.

Perhaps we need to get a little bit lost in order to find ourselves. Aune Head is a good place to start.

Only here is the tiny river called the Aune. It flows scarce a mile before taking the name Avon, continuing a beautiful journey across Dartmoor and the South Hams of Devon, ending in a wide estuary on a lovely stretch of the Channel coast. But at Aune Head, there is little suggestion of a mighty river, just a great bowl of mire, dotted with hazardous patches of bog. Your presence on its rim might cause a heron to flap clumsily skywards, for the sky is all about you, there is little ground higher, the only sound the sad and distant cry of a curlew, or the far call of skylarks.

A ruined hut lies on the very edge of the mire, just a square of granite. This was the isolated home and workplace of a medieval tin miner, who even in an age when Dartmoor was more populated than today, probably saw no other human being for weeks at a time. I can imagine how his life must have been. I once camped near his hut for just a week, seeing no one and hearing nothing but the running of water, the bleating of sheep and the cries of the marsh birds.

As night fell in my little tent I imagined I could hear the conversation of people coming closer and closer. But as I stepped outside there would be nothing and no one. Such are the ways solitude plays on the mind in lonely places. Being alone in remote countryside, away from the call of so-called civilisation, is one of the very best ways of healing a troubled mind.

Turning away from Aune Head, mostly following the tracks of sheep, or tramping through trackless heather, brings another of Dartmoor's great mires into view. Fox Tor Mire, named after a diminutive clump of rocks on its southern edge is greater in size than Aune Head, with a reputation for being treacherous. It inspired the forbidding Great Grimpen Mire of Sir Arthur Conan Doyle's novel *The Hound of the Baskervilles,* and tales are told of escaping convicts seen no more after trying to traverse its boggy acres.

From here the line of crosses marks the monastic route across the Moor. I like to stand where the stone crosses lead up on to the windswept Ter Hill and look across this to Fox Tor and the tomb of Childe the Hunter. It is said that Childe of Plymstock, caught by a blizzard one day when out hunting, perished there, despite cutting open his horse and crawling inside. Having once fought my way back to Princetown that way, in a whiteout of blinding snow, I can well believe the story, though the Childe's Tomb of today is a recent restoration of what looks like a Bronze Age kistvaen. Everywhere on Dartmoor despairing yarns are told. There is probably an element of truth in many of them.

I followed the line of crosses to the tiny, though beautiful little river known as the Wo Brook or, with the perversity of Dartmoor etymology, just the O Brook. It tumbles down amidst old mine workings to join the Dart just below Combestone Tor, through a deep valley filled with rowan trees. I have always had fond memories of this brook, since camping near to its source as a boy. The mine track to Hexworthy from the abandoned Hensroost Mine was my favoured way to refreshment at the Forest Inn, which had a bar at its rear for those too young for alcoholic beverages.

The Hensroost Mine Track winds around the side of Down Ridge through moorland and newtakes to the hamlet of Hexworthy. It is hard to believe that such an innocuous path could become the subject of a dispute ending in the High Court, but so it did. In the 1980s the landowner - the Prince of Wales - and some of his tenants summarily closed off this ancient right of way. A public inquiry was held, legal points were taken to Court, but still the path remained closed.

Some of us still used the way, despite confrontation, until the area was opened for walkers under the *Countryside and Rights of Way Act*. I was honoured to be asked to lead a walk to celebrate its re-opening, in which hundreds of Dartmoor ramblers participated. I am thrilled that future generations will be able to enjoy a path that many of us fought so hard to restore to public use.

The mine track crosses the Wo Brook by way of a charming stone bridge. I never cross it without recalling a day of thick mist when I wandered up the brook from the road at Saddle Bridge. A morning of great stillness with visibility down to just a few yards. Dartmoor mists can be a real challenge, but for the competent navigator they are often the best time to be out and about on the Moor. You feel the elemental presence of the wilderness, there is just you and nature. It is like being out of this material world.

On that day I followed the brook upstream. Walking quietly, watching the birds flit from tree to tree, and the tiny trout in the river pools. As I reached the old bridge I became aware of a loud splashing. Creeping closer I was rewarded by the sight of an otter leaping from the bridge, then dashing up the bank, and leaping in again, swimming the tiny pool, clambering back to the bridge, shaking furiously, then diving once more. It was a privilege to be there, and it was probably only thanks to the mist that I got such a close view. Such are the adventures that might be had in the wildest scenery in southern England.

~

Not all of Dartmoor is so peaceful. Its wildest northern areas remain military training grounds. Precious sites of special scientific interest battered by mortar fire, access can be restricted, despoiled by military litter and damage – and all this in a so-called national park?

On a visit to compile a report on the scandal for the Council (now Campaign) for National Parks, it took a couple of attempts to walk the highest summits in southern England. Despite being beautiful May weather with holidaymakers thronging the narrow lanes of Devon, the wildest, northern half of the Dartmoor National Park was closed to visitors - the army was in training across southern England's last great wilderness.

My initially postponed walk had to be rescheduled. I was not the only frustrated hillwalker out that day. A couple of dozen others, denied access to these high hills during the week, were thronging Okehampton's moor gate. Those great hills, Rowtor, West Mill Tor, High Willhays and Yes Tor guard this north frontier of Dartmoor in a sensational way, a rare touch of the mountains in England's over-developed south. Just beyond the moor gate a sign warns you that this is a firing range and if you touch anything you might be killed - a fine welcome in a National Park!

It is a hard ascent over one summit to another; Row Tor, West Mill Tor, the final goal being the high massif of Yes Tor and High Willhays, over two thousand feet of rocky moorland, with wondrous views across Devon to the distant Atlantic. High wild countryside is a rare commodity in these parts and the chance to go out into the wilderness a treat for everyone who loves such wild places. But as you climb the hills of northern Dartmoor, the experience of wilderness is diminished. The military has constructed a tarmac loop road into this great open space. Miles of ancillary tracks cobweb across the neighbouring heights. As I sat on the summit of West Mill Tor, a steady procession of civilian traffic began to make their way out along the military roads and into the wilds, the noise of engines and the glint of sun on windscreens bringing urban England into what should be the quiet heart of the National Park.

Looking across to the slopes of Row Tor, I could see the artificial banks of turf and metal that makes up firing targets, a weird intrusion on that rising stretch of moorland. Even on a non-firing day, military helicopters buzzed through the sky, often lower than me, adding to the noise and visual intrusion of the motor traffic. Sometimes my walk felt more like a military exercise, with occasional discarded flare cases, ration packs, sandbags and spent bullet cases clustered around the rocks. Here and there are hollows, where mortar shells have thudded into the surface of Dartmoor. Hilltops are disfigured with ugly military structures, occasionally old where some attempt has been made at concealment, but more often stark tin huts on open stretches of moorland.

Now, of course the army has to train, but I find it difficult to understand why national parks have to suffer in this way? Despite the fact that the army has shrunk in size to fewer than 100,000 troops they are hanging on to almost as much land as they had at the time of National Service, making the Ministry of Defence the fourth largest landholder in Britain. There is little logic in Dartmoor training, where training with supportive artillery is now banned, where training with supportive armour is not allowed, and where training with air support is limited, all requirements of modern warfare.

I asked an acquaintance of mine, a long-serving infantry veteran, to comment. He said "the problem is that elements of the army hierarchy are desperate for something or somewhere to command, hence all this land-grabbing. It really is absurd that millions of pounds are paid out for land at a time when front line troops are denied basic equipment and even proper food!"

He agreed with me that there should be a land audit of MoD holdings and that excess land - particularly in National Parks - should be released. I remembered that highly decorated veteran's words as I made the last long haul on Yes Tor overlooking the patchwork fields of North Devon. It is a magnificent top, but again spoiled by a hideous army flagpole and military lookouts around the rocky tor. As I walked the ridge to Dartmoor's highest hill, High Willhays, the loftiest ground in England south of the Peak District, which has been assaulted with a wide army track, both to the summit and along the great ridge itself, a stone-filled rocky road cut deep into the heart of the peat. This particular scar, marches beside the low rocks that make up the summit of Willhays.

I walked over the shoulder of Willhays, to the rocky spur of Forsland Ledge, where a massive tin hut overwhelms what should be an iconic Dartmoor view over the deep cleft of the West Okement river valley.

Writing a century ago Dartmoor's greatest guidebook author, William Crossing, remarked that this "is a picture that has not many equals on the Moor". It is still a magnificent view, but marred by a military hut and stable on the Ledge, and neighbouring huts on the opposite summit of Kitty Tor. Summing up the experience of a walk on Dartmoor's greatest hill, William Crossing says that you will look upon a picture "instinct with the spirit of Dartmoor".

Instinct with the spirit of Dartmoor.

Sadly, it is not that today, for what should be an unbroken view of wilderness is marred by man-made intrusion.

One of the wildest areas of Dartmoor is the great area of boggy moorland in the vicinity of Cranmere Pool; a hollow in the peat that is the destination of all hardened Dartmoor walkers.

I made my way there from High Willhays, via Dinger Tor. Here again civilian four wheeled drive vehicles had accessed the high ground using a military track running out from Okehampton. The journey across heather and mire was naturally hard going a century ago, when William Crossing was walking the moor.

It is harder now. A century of artillery firing has peppered the surface of the heath like lace, the shell holes giving the landscape the look of the Great War's Western Front. Fortunately, the use of artillery ended twenty years ago but, as I leapt from the edge of one water-filled hole to the next, more recent hollows, created by mortar fire, became apparent in what is supposed to be the North Dartmoor Site of Special Scientific Interest. Cranmere Pool is really just a hollow in the great northern peat bog of Dartmoor, boasting little water, yet its remoteness from civilisation is its attraction to the moorland walker.

The journey to Cranmere Pool is supposed to be one of Dartmoor's iconic expeditions. In 1854, the Chagford guide James Perrott placed a pickle jar there so that "gentlemen" might leave their visiting cards to prove that they had made the trip. In the latter years of that century this was replaced by a visitors book and the tradition began of leaving a postcard for the next walker to collect and post. I have made the journey to Cranmere hundreds of times, from all directions. But even that expedition is open to the cheats who can use the military roads to drive within a mile of the pool.

Journeying north, I reached Okement Hill. This is the southernmost point of the surfaced sections of the military loop road. In William Crossing's time it must have been one of the loneliest places in the country. On this warm May afternoon what should have been just a staging summit in the wilderness resembled a village car park, with civilian vehicles sprawled beside the military observation posts. I hurried away towards the conical hilltop of Steeperton Tor. This beautiful and dramatic summit has been disfigured by a military hut, clearly visible from the broad plain of Taw Marsh to its north.

As I walked back to Okehampton, via the Belstone Tors and Cullever Steps, past more huts, warning signs and range posts, I reflected on the surrounding stark and dramatic landscape. Just the kind of place that all hillwalkers might relish. But there is no sense of getting away from it all, as there are even on some other parts of Dartmoor. The military intrusions and the civilian traffic on the loop road diminish what should be spectacular and unspoiled. At Okehampton moor gate I read the military firing notice for the following week. For four days out of seven, this part of the Dartmoor National Park - the highest summits in southern England - would be closed to visitors.

Does it matter that the wild country of our National Parks is diminished in this way? I think it does and for the following reasons. We need wild country. It is at a premium in these over-crowded islands, and it should not be sacrificed for perceived short-term gain. Dartmoor's greatest champion, the late Sylvia Sayer, observed in her ground-breaking book *Wild Country*:

It is well understood that a proportion of people in this country are unable to feel the inspiration of the untamed hills, just as some people are tone-deaf to great music. They cannot help the lack of this particular endowment, and it is their own great loss. But there are others, many others, who experience a sense of liberation and renewal whenever they set food on wild land. Millions of quiet people do feel this. National Parks are not just a nice but slightly unnecessary luxury for a fortunate few. They are in fact a vital provision for a very real human need.

Never has the need for the preservation of wild country and National Parks been put so succinctly. Lady Sayer, for many years chairman of the Dartmoor Preservation Association (DPA), was a true visionary. I had the privilege of knowing her well and she was my inspiration when I took over as chief executive of the DPA.

Fighting for Dartmoor was the most exhausting nine years of my life, not helped by having a National Park Authority committed to compromise and sell-out, and even a DPA committee that mostly did not believe in what I came to call the "Sayer Values".

Dartmoor, of all our National Parks, has faced the greatest threats; not only from the abuse of military training, but from reservoir-building and quarrying, conifer planting and challenges to public access.

Only by rolling back such intrusions will Dartmoor deserve the name of National Park, only then will the whole of the Moor be available for quiet recreation, and Sylvia Sayer's dream of wild country be fulfilled.

~

As we emerge from the dank fir woods of Fernworthy, we know we are in for a hard time. The wind, blowing eastwards across the lonely hills of northern Dartmoor, is estimated at a steady 60 mph by the sailor in our party. It becomes hard to stand. A few yards makes every muscle ache and the screaming gale tells me to turn back...

Not that bad weather is unusual on Dartmoor. And the several miles to Cranmere Pool is considered to be a hard walk even on a calm and sunny day. We trudge across the infant River Teign and memory brings back a scene from my teens: the first visit to Cranmere, from Okehampton, that time in a thick mist, frantically clutching a compass and an ancient Ordnance Survey map. I see again the three goes it took me to find that peaty puddle with its letterbox and visitors' book – one tiny depression in the fen amid a thousand others.

Cranmere Pool is nothing special. There are more beautiful Dartmoor destinations; harder walks, too, if the truth be known. You go for it because it is there. Generations of walkers have made the trip, even before the renowned Victorian guide James Perrott started the mass pilgrimage in 1854 by leaving a pickle-jar for visitors' cards. Now a concrete letterbox serves, where you can leave a postcard for the next visitor to collect and sign a visitors' book.

That side of the pilgrimage has never appealed to me much. I like Cranmere because it can be approached from twenty different directions, each taking in some of the wildest walking in England. Over the years since that first tentative expedition, I have made the trip more than a thousand times, sometimes with company, more often alone...

The broad slope of Manga hill doesn't shelter us from the wind. Remembering I'm the leader, I glance back and see some one of the party straggling some yards behind. We wait for him to catch up and I give the option of turning back. Part of me wants them to say yes. I'm out of breath and can feel the drumming of a pulse in my ears. Doubts assail me. Would I even be able to find the place? I'm navigating off the landscape, but two of the others are checking my every move with their compasses...

The ground beneath our feet is boggy now and our boots sink several inches into the surface water as we reach the summit of Hangingstone and look out across the broad plateau of Cut Hill, Fur Tor, Great Links and High Willhays – places which bring back memories of youthful adventures.

The summit of Hangingstone is despoiled by an ugly brick and concrete shelter. I explain to my party alternatives to live-firing within National Parks. Unlike the Ministry of Defence, and Prince Charles, who takes a fortune out of the defence budget as rent for the land on Dartmoor, my people listen.

There is no shelter for us now as we head across the plateau towards Cranmere, negotiating an uneasy path between mire and shell holes. From the Hangingstone direction, the pool can be found by lining up a sequence of distant landmarks. But, even with eyes that water in the gale, I can see that one hollow amongst all the others, and warm at the thought that we will hit it spot-on, journeying the last few hundred yards from tussock to tussock, descending into the pool...

Contrary to popular belief, Cranmere is the source of no Dartmoor river, though it lies on the watersheds of the Dart, Teign, Taw, Okement and Tavy. Hundreds of years ago there was a moorland tarn at Cranmere, but now even the heaviest rain only fills one corner.

"It's all downhill from here," I shout to the others. It's not, but with the wind behind us we seem to float back across the fen to the source of the Dart. The whole mire seems to move with every step. I notice one or two anxious glances. But it's fine if you keep moving.

Down, down, down, back across the Teign and through the dark woods of Fernworthy to cars, civilisation and rest. After the wilderness, we feel uneasy about this renewed contact with the trancklements of our modern century. We stand around for a few moments, unwilling to drive and leave it all behind.

There are finer walks in Devon than the trudge out to Cranmere, but few that give such a buzz of satisfaction. Perhaps the real magic of Cranmere is that it instils in every walker a desire to keep such places truly wild.

~

At night our countryside takes on a whole new identity, mysterious and forbidding for some, challenging and exciting for those who dare to cross the threshold and venture outdoors. All through my boyhood I read avidly the tales of old time poaching in the woods of the great estates, of the darkened heaths where highwaymen lurked, and the wild coastlines where smugglers landed their cargoes after midnight. There is a long tradition of more innocent night roaming, from the naturalist in search of our more elusive wildlife to the literary man in search of inspiration. The insomniac Charles Dickens wandered the streets of London, and the country lanes around Gads Hill, from dusk until dawn, composing stories in his head.

Moonlit nights saw me meandering on Dartmoor, across a landscape that seemed unearthly, something far apart from the workaday world of the Devon towns. Nightwalking the Moor has enjoyed something of a popularity in recent years, useful as a way of teaching navigation across wild countryside. And this is not just an activity for the military. The Dartmoor explorer Ted Birkett Dixon became renowned for his group walks at night, in the last years of the old century. I led group walks on Dartmoor at night in the 1970s, though I found more enjoyment by walking alone.

Some people will argue that a rocky and boggy place like Dartmoor is difficult enough to negotiate in broad daylight. I'm often asked whether I can see anything at all, whether I am walking in total blackness. But night roaming is not walking blind. The truth is that there is a great deal of light in the countryside, particularly when the moon is full. The secret is to let your eyes become adapted to what light there is, resisting the temptation to use a torch which can ruin your night vision for many minutes. I recall one expedition walking in darkness from

Merivale to North Hessary Tor, able to see far out across the moorland, so good had my night vision become. But once across the tor, Dartmoor Prison came into view, its intensive security lights dazzling. I was almost blinded for a good half hour.

My favourite Dartmoor night walk, the one that comes to mind whenever I recall those youthful nights of exploration, was across the higher summits of the south Moor. From Bittaford I walked into the wild, climbing Western Beacon, following the ridge to Three Barrows. A warm still night, not a breeze, the only sound feet crunching on the moor grass, for there had been weeks without rain. Once into the moor, the lights of the villages and traffic faded, though over the hilltops was the glow of the city of Plymouth and flashes from the Eddystone lighthouse. It was a good clear night of stars, for the moon was not yet risen. There were the famous constellations, seeming so large that you might reach up and touch them. I lay on my back against a stone cairn on Three Barrows and watched the bright light of a satellite pass overhead.

I wandered up to Redlake and sat beside the waste tip of the old time china clay quarries. Now it has grassed over, but then it was shining white and luminous as it caught the first light of the rising moon, the great pond beneath turning from blackness to gold as I watched. I threw in a stone and watched the reflection of the moon quiver. A vixen yelped nearby, and the sheep stirred. Not a human soul seemed to be on the Moor that night, the hut circles, warreners' huts, and stone rows left to their memories and their ghosts. As the sheep settled the space around returned to an unearthly quiet, the only sounds coming when I moved on, footsteps on the heather. As I absorbed the solitude of the Moor and found an ease within it, I thought that there was no better place to be on that summer's night.

Somewhere on the long slopes of Ryder's Hill I found a badger sett. People think of badgers as creatures of woodland, but they have a great many homes on the open hillsides of Dartmoor. Their sett a great earthen fortress, surrounded by bracken, flattened where the brocks had rolled it down, permeated by a dozen paths by which the animals made their way down to the river.

Badgers tend to leave these open setts much later than they might do if surrounded by woodland. They had been long out by the time I discovered their home, but I was fortunate to see two returning from their nightly perambulations, grunting with impatience as both tried to enter a hole at the same time, the noise echoing from one side of the valley to the other. Drenched in moonlight I arrived on the summit of Ryder. Distant lights showed where there might be people, but no one was in sight. I felt like the last man on earth as I looked back into the darkness of those moorland miles.

~

Some of my most memorable Dartmoor walks have been in the mist. There is something quite magical and other-worldly about tramping through wild country when the horizons have closed down to a few yards. For all you can tell, nobody is within miles of you. Standing stones, tors, rocky river beds and round houses emerge with a suddenness that verges on the miraculous. Many walkers fear mist and will not venture out on to the Moor in all but the clearest weather.

It's true that you lose the view on misty days but, supposing you can use a map and compass with confidence, you make up for that by experiencing Dartmoor at its most elemental. In the consciousness of many who have never visited the place Dartmoor is a land of mists and mires, literature and popular perception have told them so. Most guide books have at least a few paragraphs expounding the "dangers" of Dartmoor mists, how you might get lost, how you might stumble into a bog or be benighted in the wilderness. This is all possible. The Dartmoor walker who claims never to have been mislaid in a mist has never walked very far.

If adventure is controlled risk then we should all experience walks on Dartmoor in all conditions. This does depend on the ability to navigate. I am horrified at the number of walkers I encounter who regard the compass around their neck as some kind of talisman, worn for luck and with little idea of how it actually works. Learning to use a map and compass is really easy and opens up the possibility of exploring Dartmoor in all weathers. The weather on Dartmoor can change suddenly plunging the brightest day into gloom, so it is as well to be prepared.

Experience doesn't protect you from the onset of mist. Even the great William Crossing got lost upon the Moor. In his book *Amid Devonia's Alps* he recounts a walk in atrocious weather, not just mist but driving rain, to Hexworthy, when he got badly lost and only discovered his position by falling into the old mine working at Ringleshutts Girt.

In the same chapter he tells how Mrs Hooper, then resident of Nuns Cross Farm was lost upon the Moor for many hours, going round in circles within a mile of her home. I have my own experience of being badly lost. As a teenager, walking with a former school friend, we got caught by a mist just west of Redlake. We had been properly prepared, but found that our compass had somehow fallen out of our knapsack. We wandered around, and no doubt in circles, for many hours. It was a very thick mist, visibility of no more than a few yards.

Obstacles really do become magnified in size when seen in low visibility. Every heather bush on our limited horizon took on the dimensions of a tor until it was actually reached. We found two or three times a huge mine gully of a depth that I knew simply didn't exist on southern Dartmoor. I think on reflection it was the one above Hensroost, though the mist gave it massively exaggerated proportions.

We were just considering the possibility of bivvying for the night when my friend (who was training to be a vicar) raised his eyes to heaven and cried out "oh for a sign, a sign". Almost immediately one of the Ter Hill crosses loomed out of the mist and the situation was resolved, though even I was a trifle spooked at the coincidence - if that is what it was?

Benighted travellers of old allegedly blamed their misfortune on the Dartmoor pixies. To be "pixy-led" means to be led astray. The traditional cure for breaking the spell is to take off your coat and put it on inside out. In his very readable "Hints to the Dartmoor Rambler" at the beginning of his *Guide to Dartmoor*, William Crossing suggested following a river downstream if you are badly lost, which I suppose might be better than dying of exposure. The disadvantages are that you could end up miles from where you want to be and, while you might get away with such a policy on Dartmoor, the same tactic in a mountain district could easily take you over a cliff.

Where Dartmoor is at its most ferocious is when the cloud cover of driving rain – or even snow – brings both mist and wind. This is probably the worst that nature can throw at you, though nightfall compounds the horror. Unless you are an experienced hillwalker it is better not to set out in such conditions and if you get caught up in such conditions to seek shelter as soon as possible.

But what I call the gentle mists of Dartmoor can be a treat, those still days when the mist lingers over valley and hill top. It is by such experiences that we discover ourselves, lost or not. The human spirit needs adventure and an element of risk. It is sad that our over-protective society fails to recognise such needs. Dartmoor is just the place for such adventures, but those who know it best know it in all conditions, from bright sunlit summer days and through the rain and the mist.

The Old Paths

Hidden away under the green mantle of the springtime trees, where Devon meets Dorset, I discovered an intriguing network of old paths. In 1685 the rebellious Duke of Monmouth, illegitimate son of Charles II, landed at Lyme Regis in an attempt to seize the throne. From all over the West Country labourers, many armed only with sickles and other agricultural tools, came to join his army.

Because the troops of King James II guarded the major roads into the district, the peasant soldiers took these older tracks, green lanes, hollow ways, field edges, and woodland paths, seeking a safer journey into Lyme. Many of the routes they used still exist and may be followed by today's ramblers. Some have been incorporated into the Liberty Trail, a thirty mile walk to Lyme from Ham Hill in Somerset.

Walking out from Lyme Regis I decided to march in the footsteps of Monmouth's rebels, exploring that beautiful border land where one mile you are in Devon and the next in Dorset, then back again. The stretch of coast westwards of Lyme is one of the most dramatic in England, formed by the great landslip of 1839, when a huge section of cliff tumbled into the sea, forming a great chasm that has now become a wild and tangled clifftop forest. The Undercliff, as it is known, offers some challenging walking, for the narrow path winds and dips for several miles between Lyme and Axmouth, offering no escape, except a return. It is rambling for the hardiest of walkers, the scene immortalised as the geological playground of Charles Ryder in John Fowles' novel *The French Lieutenant's Woman*.

Intending to walk inland, I followed the path into the Undercliff only as far as Chimney Rock, a tall column of decaying cliff that does indeed resemble something like a chimney, overshadowing the neighbouring trees and offering a fine view over Lyme Bay. A precipitous footpath takes the walker to its top by way of steps cut out of the hillside. It is a steep climb and I felt breathless as I rested on the stile above it. I don't know what it is, but I find the ascent of steps much more tiring than just walking up the side of a hill. It might be psychological, or just the fact that you are using a different set of muscles. I always ache more after anything resembling a staircase.

From the fields at the top are wonderful views of Lyme Regis, huddled down in a dip between decaying cliffs. Apart from Monmouth's days there, the town has a bloody history. Burned several times by French raiders, and besieged - but never captured - by Royalist forces in the English Civil War, when 500 defenders held out for Parliament against a force ten times greater. It is said that the River Lim ran red with blood as Royalist cannon pounded the town from these neighbouring hills.

We have watched such actions in my lifetime in places like Beirut and Kosovo; it is hard to remind ourselves that peaceful areas of the countryside of England were ever such battlegrounds. Just inland from Chimney Rock my walk took me along Gore Lane. When I first saw the name on the signpost, I thought this must have something to do with Lyme's bloody past, but in fact Gore can also mean a triangular piece of land. I wondered if that is a much more innocent explanation for the name of that land. I cannot find an explanation for the name of Horseman's Hill, where I wandered along a field edge before descending a lovely stretch of steep woodland, filled with bluebells. The footpath contouring the slopes of the hill offers exceptional views over Uplyme and the valley of the River Lim.

The railway travels no more to Lyme Regis, but the great viaduct at Cannington is a reminder of how Edwardian navvies carved a route through these deep valleys on the eastern edge of Devon. There is something sad about a railway line with no rails. Close your eyes and you can imagine the locomotives thundering, hearing their whistles echoing across the meadows where now cattle and sheep graze peacefully. Closing these branch lines was the height of bureaucratic stupidity. How we would have valued a train journey to Lyme Regis, how the preservation of the little stations and halts might have reduced motor traffic on our roads. Cannington Viaduct must have been a wonder of its age. I clambered up some of its antique brickwork for a better view and could not help but admire the solidity of a building enterprise carried out a century or more ago.

The countryside around must always have been favoured, for a Roman villa once stood on a nearby hilltop. Not that there is anything to see, just a mark on the Ordnance Survey map. Walking up the lane I imagined some well to do Roman, or more likely a Romanised Briton, standing by the entrance to his luxurious hilltop home, admiring a view that has probably not changed a great deal.

Uplyme is a delight, despite its busy road. Sitting in the churchyard, I thought of the novelist Henry Fielding, who became so enamoured of a farmer's daughter hereabouts that he carried her away, immortalising her as Sophia Weston in *Tom Jones*. William Wordsworth rode to Uplyme one day from his home in Dorset to order coal and was so enraptured that it wasn't until he walked home again, enwrapped in the poetic spirit, that he realised that he had forgotten his horse. As if two giants of English literature were not enough, Uplyme boasts a third, for Jane Austen liked to walk this way, commenting on the beautiful trees in her letters home.

The trees that delighted Jane enchanted me as I walked by the waters of the Lim, before following the bridleway to Whitty Hill, a wonderful airy place where I lay down in the shelter of the trees dozing in the heat of the spring afternoon.

Whitty Hill takes its name from Thomas Whitty, creator of the Axminster carpet, who built the grand house of Rhode Hill that dominates the valley nearby. Whitty was an entrepreneur of the old school and made a substantial fortune from his carpets. Perhaps the greatest reward of all must be to have a hill named after you. It certainly buys you a little bit of immortality, for I never venture on to that windswept hilltop without remembering Mr Whitty. His hill is a good place for a rest, there is the shade of trees on hot summer days, a comfortable earthen bank to lie against, and bushes to shelter you from the wind. It is so peaceful, and so little visited that I have often dozed there for hours, just listening to the sigh of the breeze in the tree boughs.

A network of old paths leads to Hole Common, now heavily wooded, but open countryside in times past. These are the tracks that Monmouth's rebels would have taken over three hundred years ago. They wore a garland of green leaves in their hats to show that they were on the side of 'King Monmouth' rather than that of James II. Most of the rebels walking these paths in that summer of 1685 never returned home; some fell at Sedgemoor, others were hanged in a score of village squares; more were transported as slaves, never to see the West Country again. Monmouth himself was butchered by the axe in the Tower of London. I thought of them often as I trod in their footsteps, wondering what sort of men they were and whether they regretted their part in this hazardous gamble for the throne.

I was now in Dorset, though the fields of Devon were in sight across the valley at the foot of the wood. Both counties may be seen from the summit of the oddly named Dragon's Hill. But in a way the border is immaterial, for this corner of England is exquisitely beautiful and much the same in mood whichever county you are in. The coast around Lyme is now a World Heritage Site, its coast path used by thousands of walkers each year, but the quiet hinterland around the valley of the Lim is less often explored. I have walked its paths often, seeing fewer walkers than in the wildest spots of Dartmoor.

The constant erosion of its old rocks is heaven for the fossil hunters who throng the beaches, seldom going away empty-handed. Fossils have been Lyme's big industry since twelve year old local girl Mary Anning uncovered an Ichthyosaur two hundred years ago, launching our obsession with all things dinosaur. This unlikely scientist lies buried in the graveyard of the parish church, and I stood by her grave for a moment or two pondering how her discovery changed the way we think about the Earth, our evolution, causing a conflict with religious faith. Out on to the sea front, a party of youngsters came along with hammers and chisels, heading for the latest coastal landslip, chattering with excitement about what fossils they might find.

Lyme is very busy these days, whatever the weather. People like Lyme, packing its beaches on hot summer days, promenading its long sea wall and staring into shop windows. It may always have been so, for it has long been a fashionable resort.

The young people were all wild to see Lyme, wrote Jane Austen in *Persuasion*. Jane was quite a fan, staying in a cottage in the town and undertaking many walks in the district. Her admirers have made the pilgrimage since, including Alfred Tennyson who, on being offered a view of the spot where Monmouth landed, muttered to his guide "don't talk to me of Monmouth, show me the place where Louisa Musgrave fell," the place being the raggedy stone steps on the Cobb known as Granny's Teeth. And Louisa Musgrave doesn't exactly fall from them in Miss Austen's tale; she jumps in a dramatic bit of attention-seeking. The Cobb, Lyme's great stone breakwater built in the reign of Edward I, features too in John Fowles' novel *The French Lieutenant's Woman*. Like its heroine Sarah Woodruff I finished my walk at its end, watching the waves sweep on to the town's sandy beaches.

The Roadside Fire

Change is his mistress, chance his counsellor;
Love cannot hold him, duty forge no chain;
The wide seas and the mountains call him,
And grey dawns know his camp fires in the rain.

The roadside fire is as much a symbol of the amateur tramp as knapsack and walking staff. Generations of vagabonds have lit fires to boil a billy of water. A time to savour, those few minutes from the lighting of the fire to drinking the tea or coffee. Watching flames as the water boils should be an act of contemplation, a break from the journey to reflect on the way you have come, the adventures you have had, the miles still ahead.

Professional wanderers on the roads of Britain call this brew-up the 'little drum'. Putting a pebble in the water tells when the water is boiling by the drumming sound it makes. When two or more tramps meet, the little drum can be quite an occasion. Stephen Graham, that pre-war advocate of outdoor adventuring, said that the fire "is part of the very poetry of the tramping life".

Drum-ups are now rare, for lighting fires is anathema to the bureaucrats of Britain. I can see why, I suppose. People have lit fires and let them get out of control. The ring of burnt ground where a fire has been can be unsightly. In other words the idiots have spoiled it for all.

My generation were taught to construct a fire properly and safely, leaving not a trace behind. Nowadays, the little drum is usually attained with the use of a camping stove. Fine, but not the same as an open fire; like bringing a suburban kitchen into the great outdoors. Byelaws hang heavily over any tramper that dares to put a match to kindling and a handful of twigs. But I think it is important that the fire making skills of wandering Britons are not lost for ever, and that whenever possible they might still be put into practice.

A roadside fire is not a bonfire, and beginners tend always to over-build. There is a place for a big fire, when you are on a long tramping tour and you need to dry your clothes and yourself after persistent rain. But to boil a billy you just need the heat of a few twigs, placed between three or four stones which serve the purpose of a rest for the can, reflecting in the heat. It is best to light your fire on stony ground, or on the sandy shore of a river or beach, so that when you have finished the remnants can be scattered into water, or any blackened stones turned over. *It is important never to light a fire on peat, as this can smoulder away for weeks before eventually bursting into flames.*

Gather your sticks and kindling as you walk, the latter the thin dry stalks from the edges of fields. If none are to be had cut thin shavings from twigs, so that they will catch the flame from your match. I know there are a dozen ways to light a fire without, and I have successfully tried most of them, but nothing beats the ease of using a match.

If you are camping out and plan to have a breakfast fire, store your sticks and kindling overnight in the dry, so that they are ready for what might be a wet morning. Light any fire well downwind of any tent. A single flying spark can devastate modern synthetic materials. Not that there should be any flying sparks from the modest roadside fire. If you are in an area where there are no stones on which to rest your billy, dig a narrow and shallow trench in the earth shallowing up towards the prevailing wind so that the flames might have some air. The billy can then be rested across the trench. Another method is to dig a bendy stick into the ground, with the billy swung on one end over the flames. It is best to experiment with fires in the garden at home if you can, before trying to build one out in the wild.

The fire burns away and the water boils. Time to rest and reflect. Some of the best moments of the wandering life, wisps of wood smoke rising through the trees, the gentle crackle of the burning twigs, and the sounds of boiling water. This is the time to rest on the turf or sit with a tree as a backrest, meditating on your walk, perhaps recording your journey in a notebook, or just resting and feeling part of nature. Doing what our ancestors have done since the time of the hunter-gatherers. Living in a way that many people around the world still live. The fire an occasional companion on your journey.

Downland

For years I'd always thought that there would be few undefiled places to walk in south east England. I'd imagined that people would be everywhere and viewpoints wrecked by massive over-development. I was wrong. Time and circumstance brought me to the South Downs, one of Britain's newest National Parks.

For a while the Downs around Arundel became the countryside through which I wandered the most. I found there almost the kind of peace of mind associated with my tramps through Scotland or northern England. The poet Edward Thomas, repeating the remarks of an anonymous traveller, claimed that "the road northward out of Arundel leads to Heaven".

I would certainly agree with such a remark, for such became my affection for Arundel Park and the banks of the River Arun that I decided to more or less repeat with variations the same walk all through the seasons of the year, so that I really might get to know it.

I'd gone to the Downs in the hope of finding a quintessential English landscape. There is, of course, no such thing. England has an unbelievable number of aspects, every view showing a different facet. But the pieces of this great jigsaw add to a very beautiful whole. Images of the South Downs were used as propaganda posters during World War Two, to remind the population just what was being fought for. Despite sixty years of over-development it is a land that can still touch the heart, one still worth fighting for.

My explorations began from the beautiful town of Arundel, dominated by the considerable walls of its castle, the home of the dukes of Norfolk. This old building dates back to beyond

Norman times, though every age since has left a mark. At a distance it resembles every child's imaginings of just what a castle should look like. Seeing it bear up out of valley mist brings to my mind Tennyson's "many towered Camelot" from his poem *The Lady of Shalott*.

In theory Arundel Park is closed on just one day a year - March 24th - to prevent the creation of new rights of way. In practice I often found gates locked across some of the best tracks on subsequent visits to the one described here. The public rights of way are, of course, open to walk on *every* day of the year.

Walking past the town's incredibly gothic nineteenth century cathedral, I entered the park by a lodge and followed an estate road. As I made my way up into the park, a red estate wagon drew up beside me. On many walks across the lands of the English aristocracy this would be the point where the estate employee would scowl and warn me off for trespassing. But here a friendly gentleman smiled, said hello, and commented on the glorious weather.

I came up to the Hiorne Tower, a miniature castle, often described as a folly, but not technically so, for it can be used for practical purposes. It was designed by the renowned Warwickshire architect, Francis Hiorne, supposedly to secure employment from the then Duke of Norfolk by demonstrating his ability to renovate Arundel Castle.

Sadly, Hiorne died just before work on the tower was completed in 1790. The tower is supposedly haunted, not by the frustrated Mr Hiorne, but by a lovelorn maiden who threw herself off its faux battlements. To the front is a vase like monument, bearing the inscription "Found in the museum at Sevastopol on the fall of the place before the allied forces by sea and land. September the 8th 1855, after one of the most memorable sieges on record."

It is strange to contemplate these long and forgotten wars. On the day of my walk British soldiers were still engaged in far away and pointless conflicts. How little the world has changed and learned in the centuries. Many warriors must have walked these Downs, right from the conflicts of the Iron Age to the present day. Looking at the blue sky over the English Channel, I thought of the young pilots of the Battle of Britain who once flew overhead, fighting for freedom in probably the only justifiable conflict in history. So many times in the chronicles of our island race have these very hills been the front line against threatened invasion. It makes walking them in peace a more humbling experience.

As my mind dwelt on the Crimea, I heard the trot of many horses and had a vision of red-coated cavalry preparing for a charge. I looked away to the edge of the down to see a dozen or more horse riders out for a gallop across the park. They were a fine sight, a bit of old England in colour and splendour, in a variety of hacking jackets. I watched as they raced down towards the castle, before walking down into the deep valley beyond. My next footpath was part of the Monarch's Way, a long distance trail that follows Charles II's escape route after his disastrous rout at Worcester in 1651.

As I crossed the valley bottom I stood for a while in awe at the stunning autumn colouring of the trees that lined the slopes. I find gazing at autumn trees a very spiritual experience. There is something about their beauty that touches a part of me that is surely beyond the physical. It reaches into whatever passes for my soul. I get a similar feeling in the early spring when the leaves on the trees are new and fresh and clean. And I got that sensation that I almost always experience on mountain summits - a huge reluctance to tear myself away.

Climbing the next steep slope I paused at each stile just so that I might look back and embrace their colour yet again. By now I was on a wide ridge of open downland, broken only by a few scattered groups of trees. Looking back I could see the waters of the Channel in the distance and taller buildings of the coastal edge. Someone had chosen the next solitary tree as a last resting place. Or so I gathered from a card wrapped against a branch, with the rhyme

High on the hill
Let my ashes lye
Neath stormy clouds
Or sun-drenched sky
Up there my heart takes wing
Just to hear the skylark sing
In sight of the rolling hills
And the sea
Let me lye in peace eternally.

I'm not usually a great fan of such funereal verse scattered across the countryside, but I rather liked that one. Not a bad epitaph for someone who has loved the great feeling of space that is given by the rolling downlands. I do not know if this is some ancient verse or was written just for this place and occasion. What I do know is that I would not mind lying for ever in such a place and accompanied by those lines.

I continued on to the top of the Down, wandering along its northerly edge, with wider views over the valley of the River Arun to Rackham Hill and the great flat area of Amberley Wild Brooks, one of the best bird reserves in England, and a landscape immortalised by the music of John Ireland. On the edge of a wood was a bench, one of those placed so often *in memoriam* of someone who had loved the view. I sat there and felt a reluctance to leave. With the great vista across the valley and the rolling Downs it was hard to tear myself away.

What is it about landscape? Given the evolution of humankind, we should look upon views of the land as purely functional, as the source of water and food and fuel and perhaps nothing more. But no, we are moved and need to take it all in to register in the memory. In times of illness and despair we wander back in our memory to such a place and such a view and, above all I suppose the peace. In the months that followed I returned again and again to that bench and felt an ease that I suspect most people in the workaday world never experience, to the detriment of the human race.

A steep path led downhill, the white chalk raw beneath my feet. Even on this dry day it was slippery and I negotiated my way with care. The slope was covered in the woodlands of some of the duke's pheasant preserves. On this spring day there seemed few of the birds around, (when I did this walk later in the year I put up over fifty) but what a beautiful sight they are and what good views you get of them thanks to their reluctance to fly.

As I descended I encountered an elderly gentleman with a grey beard struggling up the slope, his walking supplies carried in a plastic bag and an antiquated map case slung around his neck. Gasping for breath, he told me he was walking to Arundel. When I asked where he had walked from, he replied "quite a long way," smiled and walked on.

A turn in the path brought me to the great boundary wall of Arundel Park, a monumental building work for the labourers who constructed it so long before. A gate led on to the banks of the Arun. I walked upstream. It was close to this spot that

Charles II crossed the river three centuries earlier. I wondered how, given the steady flow of the river. The walk along these wooded banks was delightful, the experience heightened by the singing of birds, invisible amongst the trees and undergrowth. Occasionally, there would come the noise of ducks busy on the river. Muddy paths brought me to the grand bridge at Houghton, where I crossed the river and arrived at the outskirts of Amberley. A very attractive village, with a superb museum based in an old quarry hard by the river and railway station.

A turn along a dyke and a field path brought me to North Stoke. The place was just a farm, a few cottages, and a very ancient church. Nobody was about and it seemed to be one of those communities that time has forgotten. North Stoke's church is a delight, but it is no longer in regular use. Fortunately, it is preserved by people who care, and its wonderful constructive mix of flint and chalk, those raw materials of the Downs, creates a picture of harmony inside and out. So far away is this quiet setting from the bustle of the twenty-first century that it is not difficult to wander through the peaceful churchyard and imagine the generations who came to worship here.

I wandered past contented cattle through field paths and crossed the Arun by way of an imposing new bridge that seemed to lead to nowhere and strolled up to South Stoke church. A very friendly black cat greeted me as I wandered through the churchyard, rolling over for affection. A lady, putting up notices in the church porch, said that it was the cat from the nearby farm - spoilt by the farmer's children. She was equally welcoming to the little church and to the tiny settlement. She pointed out her cottage and told me to call in for a drink of water if I were ever passing that way again. I asked if she had always lived in South Stoke. No, she said, she had simply visited the church one day and never really left. South Stoke is more a hamlet than a village, just a farm, and a few houses clustered around the church. I thought it a delight, so peaceful and quiet, the only modern noise the occasional train on the distant railway line.

The church itself dates back to the time of the Saxons, with evidence of Norman and Early English stonework. Inside, it was a haven of tranquillity, light, airy, with that feeling of sanctity that seems to gather wherever people have worshipped for over a thousand years. I sat in one of the pews and let the peacefulness of the ancient house of worship overwhelm me. Time may have hurried by in the outside world, but here in the church, I felt I could close my eyes and hear the prayers of the medieval parishioners. How absolutely delightful to find two such historic gems as North and South Stoke's churches on one walk.

I sat in the churchyard and drank tea from my flask. The outside of the building, with its red-tiled roof along which tiny birds ran, is as picturesque as any I have seen. Its graveyard, though hemmed in by cottages, is an oasis of calm. I read some of the old gravestones, many of which seem to lean in reverence towards the east. The cat returned and tried to lie across my notebook as I wrote. I hope this friendly animal has many years of churchyard greetings ahead of it and that this beautiful area is never despoiled.

I followed the river downstream from South Stoke. The Arun is tidal and its chalk-white waters belted upstream at a rate of knots. I could imagine all of these flatlands below the Downs covered in water or frozen under ice. The joy of this ramble had been the sheer variety of scenery. The open downland, ridge paths, the cluttered woodlands, farm fields and delightful churches. And now the low lying marshlands, with a river of wildfowl. South Stoke remained within view for almost a mile, as

I looked back at each bend of the river. A path through a copse brought me to the front of an old inn called the Black Rabbit, very busy with the late lunch trade. I travelled on along the country lane, with a steep hillside to the north and the river to the south.

There is here a wildfowl and wetland centre, a series of pools as well as the river itself. Just beyond is Swanbourne Lake, now a pleasure area where people come to row boats and feed the ducks and swans. Its waters were used to drive the wheels of the mills below in medieval times, and today people can feed trout downstream. Despite being a popular tourist spot, with food and ice cream being sold in the lodge nearby, it remains unspoiled and a very attractive place to linger.

Arundel itself deserves exploration. This beautiful town, its buildings gathered around the castle walls, has so many hidden corners. Like many attractive southern towns it has become a centre for antiques and antiquarian books and is ideal for a browser like me. For a place its size it probably has more outdoor gear shops than anywhere else, and even a shop totally dedicated to the sale of walking sticks of every kind - a true ramblers' paradise. But even as I walked its streets my mind lingered back to the quiet folds of Arundel Park, the sweep of the Arun, and the lonely village churches so easily reached by footpath and quiet lane.

~

On a frozen day in February I was on the South Downs again, walking up to Rackham Hill from Burpham. The village stands at the end of a lane that is a terminus for motor traffic, but continues in several directions for those on foot or horseback.

Burpham's church was begun in Saxon times, standing hard by the earthen banks of a hill fort. Whether that was built by Saxons or Danes is subject to much dispute. In the first half of the last century its vicar was Tickner Edwardes, who wrote some delightful books on the countryside and the craft of keeping bees. Burpham is a delightful village. John Ruskin commented that he would live there if Coniston didn't exist.

I took the lane to High Peppering, passing a herd of bison in a field as I set out. These Downs are covered in antiquities, and a tumulus known as the Burgh was the first on my route. Even in February skylarks danced almost invisibly in the heights, the great sweep of downland alive with their song. The hillside was a gentle acclivity, just steep enough to make me warm up and breathe in the fresh air. The chalk was frozen hard and slippery, walking had to be done with care. I was following an ancient track, leading up from Burpham and the valley of the Arun, the important track that followed the ridge of the higher Downs.

I find it humbling, walking the ways people have journeyed for countless millennia. These tracks, now the recreational delight of walker and rider remain functional - farmers still use them. Sheep are driven here, as they have been since man first farmed the Downs. They grazed beside me, making an occasional sound to add to the singing of the larks. I watched them as the combatants of past wars, the pedlars, the pilgrims and other travellers of times gone must have done.

There is a timelessness about so much of our countryside, as though you could glance sideways and see history relived all around. In a sense you can, for the traces of the past are everywhere. Within view of these old tracks are prehistoric flint mines, field systems and burial mounds. An hour's wandering brought me to Rackham Banks, an immense earthwork of deep trenches and mighty ramparts. Its purpose is debatable, but as I sat there in a freezing breeze I could not help but consider how much work was involved in the construction.

The slight haze from the early frost had lifted. I could see for many miles. Amberley Wild Brooks were flooded, offering an irregular silver sheen in the plain at the foot of the hill. In another direction were the downs and borstals of Arundel Park, white with ice. A herd of Friesian cattle huddled together out of the wind on the leeward slope of Amberley Mount. Tearing myself away I climbed on to the ridge path running over Rackham Hill, now part of the South Downs Way national trail. Despite a height of just a few hundred feet it seemed as though I was on top of the world.

And in a sense I was for every trace of the stress which comes with everyday living had vanished.

Poet

It isn't hard to find traces of the poet Edward Thomas in the quiet village of Steep. There is a commemorative window in the parish church and his name appears on the tiny war memorial. Scattered around the wooded hangers of this unspoiled corner of Hampshire are three of his homes and the countryside which inspired so much of his verse and prose writings. On the hillside above the village is a huge sarsen stone memorial - regularly visited by his many admirers, a wonderful viewpoint over the countryside he loved so much.

It is now a hundred years ago since a stray artillery shell killed the thirty-eight year old poet as he stood at the mouth of a dugout on the Western Front. It was the opening day of the Battle of Arras, April 9th 1917. His time at Steep had inspired a huge amount of literary work; books on the countryside, biographies, walking studies and hundreds of essays, articles and reviews. This quiet rural scene was to enthuse his late flowering as one of England's greatest poets, much of his verse written in the last months before his departure for France.

Edward Thomas had not joined the army out of the usual patriotic zeal. When asked what he was fighting for, he scooped up a handful of English earth and replied 'literally - for this'. From his boyhood on the outskirts of London, Edward Thomas had longed for a country life, publishing his first essays in his teens. On his marriage he lived in Kent, before settling in the countryside high on the long ridge above Petersfield.

It was from the lovely parish church at Steep that I set out on a bright October day to walk in the footsteps of Edward Thomas. Thomas is a poet I much admire, his verse and prose work catching the English countryside in that transitional period before the massive expansion of the suburbs, and the absolute mechanisation of the farming industry. I find his verse very sad for it is, in itself, a memorial to a way of life and rural scene that has vanished for ever. His writings are an epitaph for lost England. But as I walked on the chalk paths around Northfield Wood and up through Lutcombe, a very dramatic valley with hanger woodlands all around, I felt as though time had stood still.

Edward Thomas loved to walk, though he often found the exercise tiring and hard on the feet. Unlike many walkers he enjoyed walking in the rain, as I do. But walking was not just a recreation for Edward Thomas; it was a necessary palliative which helped to stave off his frequent bouts of depression. As a depressive myself, I have always understood where he is coming from.

I swung up into woodlands of oak, beech and yew. Here were the small traces of a cottage that once stood in this quiet spot. The ruined building is the inspiration for Thomas's poem "A Tale":

Here once flint walls
Pump, orchard and wood pile stood
Blue periwinkle crawls
From the lost garden down into the wood.

Searching the chalky mud I found a small piece of blue pottery, a remnant of the life once lived by the inhabitants of this beautiful valley, and watched a dipper jump on stones in the rushing brook. The woodlands about are called hangers, and hang they do with precipitous steepness.

Hanger, what a beautifully descriptive word and one that seems to only exist in those parts of England where old woodland covers slopes of chalk. I sat for a while and read some of Thomas's poetry. Poem after poem is alive with this landscape, this bit of old England that has survived unchanged since the poet's tragic death. The path steepened and I revelled in the fast changing autumn colours, one of the wonders of the turning year, every shade of brown and yellow and red seeming to brush the blue sky from horizon to horizon. By the time my track arrived to meet the road at the top of Stoner Hill, it had become little more than a gully, buried feet down into the chalk.

It was from here that I walked away from Steep and out to the White Horse Inn at Froxfield. High on a plateau above Froxfield Thomas found the White Horse Inn, strangely hidden from the main road, a signpost in place but the inn sign missing - as it is to this day. Although it is known as "the inn without a name", it has always been the White Horse. This lonely public house inspired Thomas's earliest serious poem *Up in the Wind*, a long narrative verse of a Cockney girl marooned here by family circumstances. He describes in the poem how the inn

> *...hides from either road, a field's breadth back;*
> *And it's the trees you see, and not the house,*
> *Both near and far, when the clump's the highest thing*
> *And homely, too, upon a far horizon*
> *To one that knows there is an inn within.*

Though today the inn is better known, it is not hard to capture the feelings that inspired Edward Thomas if you sit in the dark bar by the glowing log fire, in what used to be the smithy. There is a charming carved wooden memorial to the poet who gave it such immortality. I sat there soaking up the warmth from the blazing log fire, half hearing the conversation of a couple of tweed-clad gamekeepers sitting with their spaniels against the far wall. They were discussing the respective merits of various shoots. Through the window I could see a pair of tethered horses being cosseted by their riders, who stroked their mounts with one hand and held a drink in the other.

These must have been such familiar sights to Edward Thomas, at this lonely inn out in the wilds. Even the barmaids seemed foreign to the place, though in place of the cockney accent of the girl in the poem, were the deeper tones of the far reaches of Europe.

Sitting there, as Thomas must so often have done, I felt as though I had drifted back in time and would not have been surprised if the door unlatched and Edward Thomas wandered in for refreshment on one of his long rambles.

I was reluctant to leave the warm fire, though the fine autumn day called me. In a half hour I was back on Stoner Hill, walking along Cockshott Lane, a pleasant road with just a few isolated houses, and the workshop of Edward Barnsley, the renowned furniture maker. Not far beyond is the Red House, where Thomas and his family lived from 1909-13. Edward's second home in Hampshire here at Wick Green is a beautiful red-roofed house with far-reaching views to the distant South Downs. Helen Thomas, the poet's long-suffering wife, would recall how the mist would fill the intervening valley, giving the house the feeling of a ship at sea.

It was from here that, once a week, Edward Thomas would walk down to Petersfield to take the train to London to seek new writing commissions and dine with literary friends, such as Arthur Ransome, W.H. Davies and W. H. Hudson. He seems to have been much happier in the company of his writing fellows than he ever really was at home with his wife Helen and his three children.

Walking was Edward Thomas's palliative for the black moods that often beset him and which occasionally led to rages or total despair. Once he stormed out into the night with his revolver, determined on suicide. But a walk amidst the darkened beechwoods cleared his mind. He recalled the incident in the autobiographical story *The Attempt*. The sheer volume of work Thomas had to undertake in order to make a living fuelled these anxieties. His pen was never still. Apart from country books such as *The South Country* and *The Icknield Way*, there were biographies of Richard Jefferies and George Borrow, reviews - he would often read and criticise a dozen books a week - and essays. Given this treadmill of a writing life, it is a wonder that so many of his books were so well written that they endure and are loved to this day.

Past the last of the houses, the lane became an unsurfaced bridleway of great charm, overhung with trees in the most glorious of autumn colours, smooth stretches of white chalk beneath my feet. It is not difficult to imagine Edward Thomas striding these paths in fair mood and dark.

A narrow path to my right led out on to Shoulder of Mutton Hill, a supreme viewpoint with far views across Butser Hill to the South Downs, all the woods around and below a riot of colour, all the permutations of brown and red, yellow and green imaginable. Here a great sarsen stone has been erected to commemorate the poet. It reads:

This hillside is dedicated to the memory of Edward Thomas, poet, born in Lambeth 3rd March 1878, killed at the Battle of Arras 9th April 1917
"And I rose up and knew that I was tired, and continued my journey".

Shoulder of Mutton hill is a fine place for such a tribute, for Edward Thomas knew it well and must often have lingered here.

It is easy to imagine his spirit being close by, for if the dead live again perhaps they do seek out the places they loved in life. The hill is bare now, below its summit trees, for the great storm of 1987 robbed it of many of its trees.

A steep descent brought me down to Berryfield Cottage, Edward Thomas's first home in the district and perhaps the one he loved the best. The Thomas family came to Steep so that Edward's son Mervyn could attend Bedales School on the edge of the village. Edward's wife Helen worked there to defray the expenses of living in such a place, though Thomas himself though that educational establishment somewhat pretentious.

He described this first Hampshire home, as 'the most beautiful place we ever lived in'. It is quiet and unspoiled to this day, glimpsed from the country lane alongside its long garden. After Thomas had moved elsewhere in the neighbourhood, he mourned the loss of this home whenever he passed by. I can understand why, for it enjoys the most beautiful of settings. As I walked by, a family of today was enjoying its garden, the sounds of laughter and play echoing across the valley.

It was from here that Edward Thomas gained a knowledge of the area as good as that of any local, acquired through long tramps around the district, talking to farmers, gamekeepers, Gypsies and inn keepers. All grist to the writing mill, inspiration for his rural essays and poetry.

It was a friendship with the American poet Robert Frost, then enjoying a long sojourn in England, that turned Edward Thomas from country writer to major poet. Thomas and Frost met in 1913 becoming inseparable companions.

As Europe tumbled towards war, Edward Thomas began to discover himself as a poet, encouraged by Frost, who had recognised the poetic nature of many of Thomas's writings about the countryside. But still Thomas resisted the call, having no belief in his abilities. He told his friend Eleanor Farjeon, "I couldn't write a poem to save my life!" But his friends badgered him into making the attempt, suggesting that he poeticise some of his earlier prose sketches. It is not hard to identify some of the locations for his verse. A deep valley beneath the woodland ridges inspired his atmospheric poem *The Combe*:

> *The Combe was ever dark, ancient and dark.*
> *Its mouth is stopped with bramble, thorn, and briar;*
> *And no one scrambles over the sliding chalk*
> *By beech and yew and perishing juniper*
> *Down the half precipice of its sides, with roots*
> *And rabbit holes for steps. The sun of Winter,*
> *The moon of Summer, and all the singing birds*
> *Except the missel-thrush that loves juniper,*
> *Are quite shut out...*

A very pleasant footpath led me down past some magnificent trees to Langley, a private nature reserve with ponds and a pretty tumbling waterfall, its joyous sounds an unexpected surprise. And there were more yews than I had ever seen on a single walk, with the exception of a tramp once through the great yew forest of Kingley Vale, not so far away. A mystic once told me that the yew was my 'guardian tree'. I find them fascinating, mysterious in their eternity. I suspect Edward Thomas was fascinated by the unusual sight of so many in one place.

I sat on a bench on the edge of the lane leading up to the war memorial that bears Edward Thomas's name along with so many others for a tiny village, and considered the poet in this landscape. The scene was peaceful now, on this still October day with the blue of the sky setting off the rich pageant of autumn colours.

How much more peaceful it must have been in 1915, when Edward Thomas marched away for the last time to end his existence in a landscape of muddy nightmares. Did he find, in those last moments, in the comradeship of men who loved him a great deal, a peace he had never known in the fields and hangers of Hampshire? I snapped out of such thoughts as a young man leading a black and grey horse up the lane shouted a greeting. "It seems like summer is come again." he said.

It did indeed!

Edward Thomas's last home at Steep was Number 2 Yew Tree Cottages, a semi-detached dwelling modest in comparison to his other homes at Steep. It was the reason for my visit and walk, for it was for sale and the Edward Thomas Fellowship had arranged with the vendors for it to be opened to those who love the writings of Edward Thomas.

To give some idea of how it would have been nearly a century ago, it had been stripped back to its pre-Great War condition, laid bare and open with furnishings of the period. The first room I entered, at the back of the cottage, had fine views up towards the hangers and Shoulder of Mutton Hill. It is reported that he would skip over the window sill and head for the hills when the gossip of women got too much for him.

Yew Tree Cottage was certainly a tiny house and it is easy to understand why he complained about the lack of space for him, his wife, three children, and regular guests. The main living room was most pleasant, but not very big for family and friends. Upstairs were the bedrooms used by Thomas and his wife, one for their children, and the guest room so often used by their friend Eleanor Farjeon. There was no bathroom, even up to the recent sale of the property. Just outside the side door of Yew

Tree Cottage grows old man, a descendant of the bush referred to in his poem *Old Man* which Thomas recalls

> *...I like not, but for certain*
> *I love it, as some day the child will love it*
> *Who plucks a feather from the door-side bush*
> *Whenever she goes in and out of the house.*

The child of the poem was Edward Thomas's daughter Myfanwy, a great advocate of her father's writings until the end of her long life.

In 1915 Edward Thomas marched away from Steep to become a soldier in the Great War. This new life with its regular pay freed him from regular journalism, allowing him to concentrate on his new-found gift for writing poetry. Only a handful of poems were published in his lifetime, though his reputation was secured by the publication of the rest of his work since. Apart from the memorial window in Steep church and the stone in tribute to his life and work on Shoulder of Mutton Hill, it is Edward Thomas's writings, which capture the English countryside in all its glory that remain his greatest monument and gift to all who love rural life and fine literature.

As I sat by the memorial window to Edward Thomas designed by Lawrence Whistler in the parish church at Steep, I thought back on my walk through Hampshire hangers that would have been so familiar to the dead poet. It is a beautiful stretch of countryside, worthy as the inspiration for Thomas's immortal poetry. I hope he found the peace of mind that I had enjoyed for a few brief hours.

Pilgrimage

On a beautiful spring morning I walked across the Polden Hills in Somerset on a pilgrimage to Glastonbury.

All was still and only the song of the dawn chorus broke the peace of the land, or rather the dawn chorus was part of the peace of the land. I seemed to be travelling in a world of green, for all the trees were filled with those first fresh leaves of the year. There was not the slightest breeze and no sign of life in any of the cottages. I felt at ease in the quietness of the world.

An hour or two before, when it wasn't even light, I had left behind the marshes of the Somerset Levels, the 'Sad Sedgemoor' of Thomas Hardy's poem *The Trampwoman's Tragedy,* where so many west country men had died on that July day of 1685, when the Duke of Monmouth's rebellion had come to such a bloody conclusion. That battle had been fought mostly in the dark and I almost sensed the rattle of the muskets and the crash of the cannons as I wandered by. It was to these same Polden Hills that the luckless Monmouth had fled after the rout, on an escape across southern England that was to lead only to the executioner's block in the Tower of London.

But my journey was without hurry and absent from fear.

Sometimes when I walk in this solitary way my feelings are interrupted by memories of music. Like most people I have my favourite composers and beloved pieces. This day it was Vaughan Williams' *Fantasia on a Theme of Thomas Tallis,* that beautiful composition which brings together two of England's greatest composers, spanning the centuries in a collective work of genius. It seemed very appropriate on this lovely morning and I fancied I could hear the music all around me in the still of the air.

As I was walking towards the ruined abbey at Glastonbury the religious overtones of the music seemed to uplift my spirit and carry me on to a plane far removed from the prosaic and materialistic modern age. I felt in harmony with an older time and much the better for that.

From a round hilltop on the edge of a wood I caught my first glimpse of Glastonbury Tor rising magical and unearthly out of the great wet plain before me. Once upon a time Glastonbury was an island, the Avalon of British myth, where King Arthur was taken to die - or perhaps to live again.

Glastonbury is to this day a strange and ethereal site, somehow not quite of this world, a place where real life and dreams seem to mix. In all my times there I have felt myself healed somehow, refreshed and inspired.

For the religious it is supposed to be one of the holiest locations in England indeed, if you accept the claims of those who have fall under its spell, the world. It was to Glastonbury that Christ was supposedly brought by his uncle Joseph of Arimethea. It is said that Joseph planted his staff on the green slopes of Wearyall Hill and watched it transform into the magical Glastonbury thorn tree, which still blooms every Christmas. Historically, there may be a grain of truth in all of this, for Joseph was a renowned merchant and there was certainly trade between the west country and the middle east two thousand years ago. And it was below the slopes of Wearyall Hill that I met Flint in his travelling wagon.

It was some two years since I had first encountered Flint and his family, when I found myself adrift in Savernake Forest. They had found me and given me shelter in their wagon. I spent a few days in their company before being sent on my way, courtesy of a friend of theirs who owned a lorry. I never quite worked out whether Flint had Gypsy blood, but his wife Amelia certainly did. Flint was a traveller, that is the best description, and when I met the family on that wild night in the forest they were in an encampment of at least a dozen other wagons. Flint was perhaps thirty, head shaven and slight, with a ring in each ear.

He looked up with a broad smile as I drew level with him as he led the horse off the road. "Well, I never thought I'd see you again. You going far?"

I told Flint where I had walked from and asked after his family.

"There's just me and Amelia at the moment. She's gone ahead into the town. We're selling her wooden craftwork at a fair. We might see you there. It's harmonic convergence day!"

"What?"

"Ah, well," said Flint. "A tribe of native Americans have decreed that this is the day that the universe harmonises the world. And Glastonbury is supposed to be the epicentre of change that will enrich the human spirit. Glastonbury Tor at Midday - that's where it all starts."

"And you believe all of this?" I asked.

"Well, I've seen stranger things happen in all my years on the road," he replied. "Perhaps I'll see you up on the tor and we can find out?"

I waved farewell and headed into the centre of the town, wandering through the remnants of the great abbey of Glastonbury, a place of pilgrimage for two thousand years or more. Since the Dissolution it has lain in ruins, but very atmospheric ruins at that. In its day, Glastonbury Abbey was possibly the finest ecclesiastical site in England, worthy of the pilgrims who would walk hundreds of miles to see its splendour and to pay homage to the remains of the saints buried there.

Legend decrees that the original wattle church was built by the carpenter Jesus himself on his visit to the island. It was this tradition that inspired William Blake to write the poem which begins 'And did those feet in ancient time walk upon England's mountains green'. This original building was incorporated into a later building which was destroyed by fire in 1184. Most of the present walls date from after that time.

And in the very heart of the abbey is the grave of King Arthur and his wife Guinevere. Or so they say. Now it is more than possible that a warrior king of the Dark Ages might be buried in such a hallowed spot. It makes a lot of sense. But the finding of King Arthur's bones in medieval times came at a time when the abbey needed money rather badly, and the best way for an abbey to ensure a ready supply of solid income was to make themselves a focus point for pilgrims. And what might pilgrims want to see quite as much as the last resting place of a legendary and romantic king?

All that is known for certain is that in 1190 the monks excavating the site of the original abbey, after the disastrous fire, found a leaden cross set into a stone slab with the Latin inscription *Hic jacet sepultus Inclitus rex Arturus in insula Avallonia* (here lies King Arthur in the Isle of Avalon.) Below this were discovered two bodies in the trunk of a hollowed oak tree. The man was very tall with a number of wounds to his skull; the fair hair of the female body crumbled to dust when touched.

In the presence of Edward I, the bodies were reinterred in front of the high altar, and the site of this grave is marked to this day. Now, cynics have suggested that the discovery of Arthur's body was very convenient for the clerics who were hard-pressed for money to rebuild the fire ravaged building. But if the Arthur burial was just a commercial gimmick, I find it strange that the monks did not exploit it more at the time. Medieval Glastonbury was advertised across Europe more for its saintly relics than as the resting place of the once and future king. It may sound an incredible con on paper, but when you are there, amongst those sacred stones, looking through the great arches of the old abbey up to the mystical Glastonbury Tor, it is not so hard to believe.

In the quietude of that early morning I could almost hear the chanting of the long-vanished monks. Such is the spell of this ancient and evocative site.

The monk's stratagem certainly worked, for Glastonbury remains a place of pilgrimage to this day. People travel from all over the world to visit the town, albeit now mostly members of the new age community. As I walked up the street I passed a number of shops selling crystals, dowsing rods, and books on magic. The heart of these new beliefs, which have by and large replaced the old Christianity (though that too has its locations here in the shape of Christian retreats), seems to be based on a reverence for the land and the planet, and no harm in that.

Both faiths seem to meet in the peaceful gardens around the Chalice Well, supposedly the place where Joseph of Arimethea hid the Holy Grail, the cup Christ used at the Last Supper. Whether the Grail was a real cup or something more symbolic is debateable. Local scholars argue that it might be a clue to an understanding of life itself. The Chalice Well flows its daily spring of twenty-five thousand gallons of chalybeate water across the beautifully kept garden, and drinking its liquid with its rich iron taste is supposed to be very beneficial to health.

To sit in the gardens is to experience a feeling of great peace, despite the rumblings of modern traffic. High above is the mighty tor, the keystone of this spiritual landscape. I remember looking up at it from the gardens at the break of day on another

May morning. The charity that protects the Chalice Well had organised a Mayday dawning event to greet the spring and I had gone along to see what might happen. Hundreds of pilgrims and locals turned up. There was a bonfire to illuminate the initial darkness, the high flames of which the braver and fitter jumped, and then the light of dawn swept across this great island in the marshes and the pilgrims sang Jerusalem and other songs that celebrate the beauty of the Earth.

I supped the waters of the old spring, waters that are supposed to travel here from many miles away, perhaps even from the distant Mendip Hills, and soaked up the tranquillity of a place that stands at the heart of British legend, that has inspired great writers such as Blake and Sir Thomas Malory. Perhaps, I considered, there is a Grail and I was within yards of it, as I smelled the flowers and sipped the water. Certainly, over long decades, Glastonbury has always called to something in me that might be my soul.

Refreshed from my rest I climbed the tor, capped with its old church tower. It was on the summit in 1539 that Abbot Richard Whiting, the last master of the grand abbey was butchered for refusing to accept the destruction of his way of life. But the top never feels to me as though it hosts bad memories, only imparting to me a feeling of permanence and peace. I have stood there so many times, alone and in company, and in all weathers.

The view is wonderful, all across the levels of Somerset to the Polden and Mendip Hills. In the far distance is Cadbury Hill Fort, the Camelot of Arthurian fable. I have seen this high ground surrounded by water after flooding, reminiscent of what it must have been when it was a true island, perhaps really the Avalon of myth, for Avalon only means apple, and apples grow there still. All around the tor are earthen terraces, perhaps man made, forming a kind of rising pathway that people still thread their way around in order to summon up magic, or take as a life journey. Some journeys around its course have culminated in memorable storms, as though threading the maze of paths has let loose the wild energies of nature.

A couple of dozen people sat or lay across the summit of the tor waiting for the moment of harmonic convergence. All was still and peaceful, hardly a breeze to move the wispy clouds across a sky of very deep blue. I asked one such pilgrim, a man of indeterminable age with long and knotted red hair what he expected to happen?

"Nothing that we'll see," he replied. "There are thin places on the surface of the Earth where the boundaries between the physical and spiritual worlds are almost non-existent. Glastonbury exists in both worlds at once, which is why this is the place to be when the harmonies of the universe converge. By being here we are twice-blessed and become the leaders of the New Age".

I felt dubious about the concept of leadership in a supposed 'new age', but the pilgrim had begun to meditate and I felt no desire to disturb him with such philosophical quibbling. Instead I waited for the moment of harmonic convergence. When the appropriate time came and passed, I do admit to feeling a deep sense of peace, ease and contentment. But then I often do when I am in such places. The other pilgrims gasped with pleasure as though experiencing some orgasmic joy that was denied to me. But I did feel rejuvenated and energetic as I left them all behind and walked down from the tor.

It reminded me of a time on Dartmoor when I walked up to the Nine Maidens stone circle from Belstone. I had been unwell and was exhausted by the time I had made the modest climb out on to the edge of the moorland. Someone had given me a pair of copper dowsing rods and I had them in my rucksack. So I dowsed the stone circle in a way I had seen others do. The rods, very obligingly, dipped and crossed in a most fascinating way.

After just a few minutes I felt strange, curiously light headed, as though I was moving about in a dream. From feeling ill, I suddenly felt miraculously well. More than that, I felt an incredible boost of energy. I positively flew around the rest of a long and difficult trek, feeling no tiredness at all as though I had absorbed some mighty power from the circle.

There are so many things that we do not understand about the Earth and the universe that I do not dismiss out of hand any possibility. Living so close to nature as I do on my solitary walks I feel that it is possible to experience a sense of union with the matter and space around me.

As I descended Glastonbury Tor, I recalled the story of the Welsh saint Collen who in the Dark Ages lived in a lonely cell at the foot of the tor.

It is said that one day a messenger came to him from Gwyn Ap Nudd, Lord of the Underworld, bidding Collen to meet his master on the peak. Equipping himself with holy water Collen clambered up the tor to find himself in a magnificent hall of gold, filled with angelic beings and beautiful music.

Resisting the temptations of the underworld Collen flung the holy water across the hall and the illusion faded away, leaving the saint alone upon the summit of the hill. This brings to mind the legend that Arthur and his Knights sleep within the hill, waiting for a time when England might be imperilled. There are many local stories of people who have followed the rushing chalybeate waters deep inside the tor and come out mumbling of the wonders they have seen. For me the wonders of Glastonbury Tor lie all around in a splendid and sacred landscape.

On the verge of the land that runs around the tor I found Flint and Amelia sitting on the steps of their travelling wagon. I told them about the people on the summit of the tor, and my own feelings of connection with the earth.

"Well, you see, I think you've got it right." said Flint. "It seems to me that if you are not converging with the Earth every moment you are out in the heart of the countryside, then you never will for a brief few moments on the summit of Glastonbury Tor."

I sat drinking tea with them for a while.

"Have you seen Gog and Magog?" asked Amelia. "Most visitors to Glastonbury miss them."

"Gog and Magog?" I inquired. "Weren't they giants in folklore? Aren't they hills near Cambridge?"

"Both of those, but the Gog and Magog I mean are two mighty oaks in the fields over there," she answered pointing to a footpath sign and a path leading away from the tor. "A very peaceful spot for a nap on a hot afternoon like this."

"I'll go and look."

"Or you could come with us?" Flint said. "Just like old times. We will do a circuit of England and Scotland and be back here this time next year."

For a moment I was enticed at the thought of regaining the outdoor life I had led in my youth, when I had walked for weeks at a time, halting and sleeping where I might, never knowing from one day to the next where I could be by sunset. It was a great temptation, the greatest for me in so many ways. But no. I had responsibilities. There was ill-health in the family and I could not be away so long. I explained my difficulties to the travellers.

I waved farewell, and left the two rovers to the crowd which was descending from the tor and starting to browse amongst Amelia's wooden craftwork. As I crossed on to the footpath I looked back at the gaily painted wagon and wondered when I might see them both again. Nobody was about as I struck out across the meadows, and the hubbub of voices was quickly left behind.

I found the trees on the edge of the track and great oaks they were. The sun was hot and I sought a quiet stretch of a meadow where I might lie down and rest, for I had had an early start and quite a long walk.

There's a lot to be said for dozing in quiet corners of the English countryside, especially on balmy summer afternoons when the bees hum above the flowers in the long grass, and there is scarce a breeze to disturb the high flight of the skylarks.

Lying on the dry ground I felt so pleasantly tired that I easily drifted into that wondrous state between sleep and consciousness, when the mind seems to float free above the earth. I found in these relaxing hours possibly more peace of mind than that entire transcendental multitude on top of the tor. All care and responsibilities seemed to vanish for a while, as the workaday world with all its entrapments and restrictions faded away. I looked up into the deep blue of the sky and felt warmth and a glow, my head reeling with the heady scents of nature, and only natural sounds all about. Time seemed irrelevant and I felt that I might lie there for eternity.

I thought of Saint Collen finding a hall of gold on Glastonbury Tor. Perhaps it was *this* feeling of absolute ease that he experienced, which became translated in legend into a more obvious temptation, the scattering of the holy water a necessary way of dragging himself into a harsher world. I thought of my travelling friends, whose life was not always a bucolic idyll, but rather a lot of hard work as they scrabbled for a living, combating those who so badly misunderstood their peripatetic way of life. Yet I knew that they must have moments of absolute ease such as mine on the hillside not far from Gog and Magog.

And I thought of the billions of people who never would, slaves effectively, who might all benefit from the freedom of the wild in such a way and be enriched. In the first still moments of the evening I put on my knapsack and began the long walk home, seeing the tor looming out of the mist for many miles as I lingered by any gateway that offered me a view.

Lavengro

Tucked away in an alleyway in Norwich is what was once the childhood home of that most neglected of English writers, George Borrow.

The author of *Lavengro* and *The Romany Rye* is scarcely read these days, his books darting in and out of print. Yet a century ago he was an undisputed influence on a whole generation of country walkers, the subject of a dozen or more biographies and scores of learned essays.

The early years of the twentieth century were something of a renaissance for the "Gypsy Gentleman". His first moment of great fame came in 1843 with the publication of *The Bible in Spain* which, despite its deadly title, is a rollicking tale of adventure describing Borrow's journeys around the Peninsula during the Carlist Wars. For a moment in time Borrow was the most famous writer in the land, his exploits praised in Parliament by the Prime Minister, and his book a bestseller. But his later fictionalised autobiographies *Lavengro* and *The Romany Rye*, failed to catch the public mood, and Borrow found his reputation eclipsed.

It could be argued that it was the recreational walking industry that gave Borrow's reputation a new lease of life around the beginning of the last century. Tales of romantic adventure on the roads of England in the days of stagecoaches, encounters with Gypsies and tinkers, and Borrow's early struggles as a Grub Street journalist, appealed to those who sought the great outdoors as an escape from the growing blight of industrial Britain.

Borrow was born in 1803, the son of Cornishman Thomas Borrow, who had fled the Duchy after a riotous brawl, but in later years become respectable as a religiously pious army recruiting officer during the Napoleonic Wars. Borrow's mother was a wayward Norfolk girl called Ann Parfrement, and some have argued – with little evidence - that George Borrow was really the by-blow of a Gypsy lover and not Thomas Borrow's son at all. Borrow certainly had an affinity with Gypsies, in boyhood becoming the blood brother of Ambrose Smith, immortalised in *Lavengro* as Jasper Petulengro.

For much of his childhood, George led a wandering life, on the march with his father's regiment. As a result he became a considerable walker capable of covering sixty miles a day. He was also something of a linguist, fluent in a couple of dozen languages.

Settling in Norwich he was an unwilling pupil at the Grammar School hard by Norwich Cathedral's Erpingham Gate, staining his face with walnut juice so that he might seem more the Gypsy, and leading his fellow students into trouble. Borrow agreed to be apprenticed to the law, but spent a good deal of time roaming the countryside and studying languages. On the death of his father in 1824, he headed for London determined to secure a reputation as a writer, failed, and took to the roads, first as a relatively respectable traveller, and then as an itinerant tinker, meeting up with his friend Jasper Petulengro and his family.

George Borrow had fallen out of favour once more by the time I discovered his writings as a teenager. But even then he was still anthologised and referred to in books by the older generation of writers about walking. I found a great delight in his work, which has remained with me to this day.

I had had quite a Borrovian childhood myself, roaming the land, and could recollect my own youthful encounters with Gypsies. It was mostly because of its George Borrow associations that I went to Norwich to read for a university degree. I can well remember my interview day, when on a darkened afternoon I glimpsed Borrow's home for the first time, and gazed longingly up at Mousehold Heath, where Borrow had so often met up with his Gypsy friends. In time I was to explore all of these Borrovian locations.

Perhaps the most relaxed time for an undergraduate are the days after the finals examinations, but before the day of judgement when the degree results are posted. In this happy month there is no work to be done and the student might enjoy a glorious holiday, free of care. Looking back I think of mornings spent walking the banks of the River Yare in the footsteps of George Borrow, a desire to be alone to reflect on the happy three years that were now the past and trepidation as to what insecurities might be to come. I would walk out to the bridge by way of Earlham Hall, then the university's school of law but, in Borrow's time, the home of the Quaker and social reformer Joseph Gurney, the brother of the prison reformer Elizabeth Fry. It was in a river pool below the hall that the young Borrow would swim and fish, delighting in the atmosphere of that restful place:

Pleasant is that valley, truly a goodly spot, but most lovely where yonder bridge crosses the little stream. Beneath its arch the waters rush garrulously into a blue pool, and are there stilled for a time, for the pool is deep, and they appear to have sunk to sleep. Farther on, however, you hear their voice again, where they ripple gaily over yon gravelly shallow. On the left, the hill slopes down to the margin of the stream. On the right is a green level, a smiling meadow, grass of the richest decks the side of the slope; mighty trees also adorn it, giant elms, the nearest of which, when the sun is nigh its meridian, fling a broad shadow upon the face of the pool; through yon vista you catch a glimpse of the ancient brick of an old English hall.

I sat in the same spot one morning, reading that account of that scene from *Lavengro*. Little had changed, though there were fewer elms after the devastation of Dutch Elm Disease. The view of Earlham Hall seems much clearer than in Borrow's time, though the smiling meadow can be walked and enjoyed to this day.

In an amusing scene from *Lavengro*, Joseph Gurney walks down to remonstrate with the young Borrow for leaving fish to gasp to their deaths on the bank. Not a word about the fact that Borrow is actually poaching and trespassing, such was the libertarian nature of that particular landowner. Indeed, Gurney must have seen something unusual in the character of the interloper, for he invited Borrow to the hall to use the library.

The young Borrow was too shy to do so then, though in his respectable middle age he did visit Joseph Gurney at Earlham Hall. As I lay back and dozed in the sunshine of that early summer morning a century and a half later, I felt that I could almost hear the conversation between the pair; the gentle Gurney and the strange youth.

I wandered down the Yare along a stretch of riverbank that seemed quite wild and unspoiled for countryside so close to the burgeoning city of Norwich.

Whatever other undergraduates were doing that day, they were certainly not walking in the footsteps of George Borrow, for no one was in sight as I paused to watch the ducks head out from the rushes to the midst of the gently flowing water. I imagined Borrow heading the same way on a circuitous route back to his home. He was tall, well over six foot, with the sturdy build of a boxer. There was a caste in one of his dark eyes, and his hair, though dark, had turned grey by the time of early adulthood. Even as a young man he was marked out by the people of Norwich as something of an eccentric.

He mixed with the wrong people for many tastes, fought practice rounds with John Thurtell, a local prize fighting promoter who was hanged for murder in 1824, and probably imbibed a lot of liquor with the Norwich scholar and renowned atheist William Taylor. Just the sort of company that made the respectable Captain Thomas Borrow shudder.

The wild countryside that Borrow would have known is intruded upon by the strange ziggurats and other buildings of the University of East Anglia, which overlook the river as it winds down to Cringleford. The concrete blocks of the university are not pretty and I suspect no one would ever say that they were, but they grow on you and have a kind of charm if you live among them for long enough.

The real joy of the place is The Broad, a great stretch of water situated between the Yare and the campus. Not that Borrow would have known it, for it only came into existence in the 1960s, when the university allowed gravel to be extracted from its lands, in what must have been a noisy nightmare for UEA's earliest students. But the pain of having a quarry there was soon eclipsed by the creation of a lovely stretch of water. Walking round I halted every few yards, as more and more wildfowl caught my eye, for The Broad is now the university's very own nature reserve. I liked best the Great Crested Grebes, swimming along with their young on their backs. Sometimes man can interfere with nature and get things right. After all, the Norfolk Broads are largely man-made and have a beauty beyond belief.

From Cringleford I walked across the city to Mousehold Heath, a place that holds considerable memories of George

Borrow. Despite the now encircling city suburbs, Mousehold (the locals call it something like Muszle) remains an oasis of wild countryside, a taste of what it was in the days when Borrow roamed its lonely heathland and wooded vales.

It was here that the Gypsies camped when they came for the Norwich fairs, and here that Jasper Petulengro taught Borrow the Romany language. Some of the memorable passages in *Lavengro* describe the heath and the view to the city below. One day the severely depressed Borrow wandered on the heath seeing little point in an existence trapped in the workaday world of Norwich. Jasper Petulengro meets up with him and, in one of the great passages of English literature, reminds him of the joy of living

"Life is sweet, brother."

"Do you think so?"

"Think so!- There's night and day, brother, both sweet things; sun, moon, and stars, brother, all sweet things; there's likewise a wind on the heath. Life is very sweet, brother; who would wish to die?"

"I would wish to die-"

"You talk like a gorgio - which is the same as talking like a fool - were you a Rommany Chal you would talk wiser. Wish to die, indeed! A Rommany Chal would wish to live for ever!"

"In sickness, Jasper?"

"There's the sun and the stars, brother."

"In blindness, Jasper?"

"There's the wind on the heath, brother; if I could only feel that, I would gladly live for ever..."

And it was this 'wind on the heath' philosophy which inspired those early Borrovians, seeking escape from the stifling indoor world of Victorian and Edwardian Britain.

The passage has inspired a great many walkers since, though few would have covered as much ground as Borrow. He probably spent several years of his early adulthood on the roads of England, travelling with Gypsies and tinkers, before assuming an almost instant respectability as an agent of the British and Foreign Bible Society, distributing testaments in Spain, and writing the accounts of his adventures that made him famous.

In later years he undertook long walking tours in Wales, Cornwall, Scotland and the Isle of Man, though only one of these expeditions led to a book, *Wild Wales*, for by that time Borrow was out of favour with the reading public.

Like many of us who love the outdoors, Borrow felt trapped in domesticity, often breaking out to roam the countryside. His long-suffering wife remarked that he would mutter over breakfast "I'm just going for a walk, dear!" and then disappear for weeks or months on end. In a lonely old age his tall dark figure might be seen drifting along the lanes near to his home at Oulton Broad, or visiting the Gypseries close to London, but his day had past, and his reputation was not to revive in his lifetime.

He died in 1881, and I often wonder if, in those final moments, his mind turned to those happy days by the River Yare or on Mousehold Heath with his oldest friend Jasper Petulengro.

Now George Borrow is out of favour once more, though he still has his admirers, and there is a thriving George Borrow Society. It may well be that we live in too material an age for a writer of such simple joys to be appreciated. For Borrow wrote as though the nineteenth century had never happened, his spirit and style yearning for the simpler eighteenth century world of his hero Daniel Defoe; an England where Gypsies could live a nomadic life, and where stagecoaches plied the roads, their horses tended by ostlers in country inns; where the talk was all of prize fights, and pickpockets and thimblerigs haunted the crowds at country fairs.

Certainly, there were no Gypsies on Mousehold Heath that day, no, nor any ostlers or thimble riggers. The world seems to have lost a lot of its colour and zest for life since the time when Borrow strode the pathways of Mousehold. I think that that is one reason why I love Borrow's writings so much. The world of today seems grey by comparison. And that is why I seek escape in the depths of our countryside, those bits of the world that have changed the least.

~

I sat on a wall up from the sea at Aldeburgh in the dark of a November evening. All along the strand and close to the restless swell of the water were a line of fishermen, their lanterns tiny suns lighting up the immediate area around where each individual sat, then a long stretch of darkness before the illumination of his neighbour. I had had too much to drink in the conviviality of Dave's Bar, and had wandered out to sober up.

That day had been a day of poetry, for we had come to Aldeburgh for its first ever poetry festival. Later, in Dave's Bar, everyone seemed to be a writer. I sat at the bar with someone who claimed to have been a friend of Dylan Thomas in his heady London days. He told me that he might have been a great writer himself, but it never happened. Inspired, I went out into the darkness, sat on the wall, and wrote a poem about Aldeburgh at night. I have it still and like it, though composing poetry is a real skill that has passed me by. With a few undergraduates, all budding fellows of the pen, we had come down for this weekend.

We were staying in the Youth Hostel at Blaxhall, once the village school, and the home of oral historian George Ewart Evans, whose work I admired. It has been renovated since, but was then simpler in concept, the way youth hostels were originally supposed to be. I'd woken early that day, strolled into the hostel's porch for a cold shower, and sat on a bench for a while, admiring the quiet East Anglian countryside. I realised as I rested there that I was completely happy for the first time in years.

That morning we walked amid the rushes and mud flats of a countryside that is as much water as it is land. The path we took passed ancient hedgerows and wound by delightful patches of woodland. The salty tang of the sea drifted inland on the gentlest of breezes. It was a landscape like no other I had explored. It may have been November but it was a balmy morning, more like the warmth of late spring. There were half a dozen of us and, much as I dislike walking in groups generally, I felt at peace in their company. We were all undergraduates, and all had a love of literature in common.

As I sit writing this nearly thirty years have passed, but that perfect day on the marshes, and that inspiring evening in Aldeburgh lives on in my heart and mind. I often wonder what became of all the others who shared that weekend, for as is the nature of these things we scattered on graduation and lost touch. I remember them well and feel grateful to them for making this loner so very welcome.

I sometimes wonder if the ghosts of our younger selves still walk those paths we took on that East Anglian day; whether the echoes of our talk and laughter may still be heard on quiet days, amongst the reeds and swaying trees. For I've come to think that we do, perhaps, leave remembrances of ourselves in the ether, in places lost and days past. It may be that no moment in time is gone for ever.

Even in mortal terms, I can close my eyes and summon up that happy day. And that is the ultimate reward of roaming through wild and lonely places. We live at a different level to the one that imprisons us in an alternative unimaginative and workaday world.

Step out and you live and are free.

Maps

The pilgrims of old didn't have much in the way of maps to guide them to the sacred shrines of medieval England. The average Briton rarely travelled from home, so there would have been little need for detailed guidance. In latter times everyone knew where the great highways of the country led, aided by the numerous milestones that marked their course. Only in the nineteenth century did the land of Britain became well mapped, and then for the purpose of possible military defence. The Ordnance Survey, originally a branch of the army, has been with us ever since, despite the moans of some cost-cutting politicians.

Britain is one of the best mapped countries in the world and poring over Ordnance Survey maps is a joy unto itself. I have always loved maps, even of places I might never visit. From the contours I can visualise whole landscapes. But when I walk I rarely glance at a map, perhaps during a halt, or when I want to name a hill or farm. I prefer to navigate from the feel of the countryside, spotting the line of the ancient footpath wending its way across fields, or working out the best way to traverse a mountain ridge. I seem to be different from a lot of ramblers that I know, whose eyes rarely stray from the map. The best walk they have ever read is the phrase that comes to mind.

As a young boy I didn't even appreciate that the countryside *was* mapped. I learned those Staffordshire and Warwickshire acres from memory, progressing a little further each time, until the territory lived in my mind. I never tried to write it down, though perhaps I should have done.

We say that people know somewhere "like the back of their hand". *That* was how I knew the country of my childhood, through constant exposure to its many wonders: from the canal towpath to the ruined farmhouse, from the harvest field to the railway line. Once that landscape was fixed in memory I could go on to the next district and the distant land beyond that. It is the way our ancestors grasped the 'lie of the land'. Years later I purchased an old map of that corner of Staffordshire and was quietly satisfied at how accurately I had mapped the place in my head.

Exploring without a map can lead to unexpected delights. You get the real thrill of the pioneer, as you come across the lake you never knew existed, the bluebell wood that you never want to leave behind, the old Pele tower guarding a border valley.

In later childhood I explored the countryside around a Devon holiday resort, in the way I had roamed the Midlands. Not buying a map, but just discovering a mile further each day. On one occasion, the end of my walk was the brow of Little Haldon Hill. I spotted what looked like a disused road quarry a mile away, looking sufficiently remote to be the end of the next day's adventuring. Once there I lit a fire and made tea, the blue wisp of smoke rising into the clear summer sky. So unspoiled did it seem to be that I felt myself in the middle of nowhere. Only afterwards, climbing up the slope, did I find the country lane above. The feeling of remoteness shrank with the first car, regained only by trespassing through the secluded and wooded country beyond.

Sometimes I would make maps of countryside explored in this way, marking the line of the roads, the green of the woodlands, and the deep valleys. I would give places names that seemed appropriate. Passing a copse I heard a woodsman chopping down a tree, so that became Cutter's Wood. Interestingly, the wood has no name at all on the Ordnance

Survey map and a local farmer told me he had forgotten the local name used by his father and grandfather.

I suppose I was influenced a great deal by the children in Arthur Ransome's wonderful series of *Swallows and Amazons* novels, who were for ever exploring areas of the Lake District and East Anglian landscapes and drawing maps with great proficiency, adding their own names to places. Ransome's books must have influenced a great many British hillwalkers and are as readable today as when they first appeared. Certainly a fair portion of my love of outdoor adventure dates back to my first readings of the Ransome canon. Whether today's ramblers should even attempt to get to know hill districts without a map is debateable. Even proposing it will probably incur the wrath of mountain rescuers, though I would suggest that very experienced hillwalkers might care to give it a try, perhaps carrying just a compass so that a course might be steered for the nearest road or river if a fog comes down. However, I see no reason why a stretch of lowland countryside might not be explored in such a way, but even then with great care.

When I came to explore Dartmoor, my first great wilderness area, I certainly had a map, but I still approached my discovery of its heather acres in much the same way, getting to know a part of the Moor adjacent to a road, then the next mile to, say, a river, then the area next to that. Using this method I soon got to know all of the hills when seen from every possible direction, the course of the rivers and the thousands of antiquities left behind from the Bronze Age and the later tin-miners.

My Dartmoor walks led to battles by correspondence with the Ordnance Survey, for some of their early maps showed a number of errors. One was over Cosdon Hill, one of the greatest heights of the northern moor, which bore the prissy name

Cawsand on the sheets produced in the nineteen sixties. There was a kind of excuse for this blunder, for local people might pronounce the hill's name as 'Cosson'. But variations of 'Cosdon' were how it appeared in documents dating back to 1240, and that was good enough for me. After a very lengthy exchange of letters the Ordnance Survey conceded the point and today that lovely summit appears on the map as Cosdon Hill.

But what was unforgivable was the Ordnance Survey's removal altogether of many local place names, there for all to see on the 1:25000 scale maps in the nineteen fifties, but not on today's much more expensive sheets.

Bad enough that the maps have become 'metricated' and that our lovely summits, once measured in thousands of feet, are now in metres, seeming dwarfed in comparison.

Despite all of these misgivings, maps are lovely creations and one of the great joys in life is to pore over a map as you prepare future expeditions, or recall the exhilarating tramps of yesteryear.

Pennines

There are some places that haunt your mind even if you have never walked there. The spectacular cut in the edge of the Pennines known as High Cup Nick is one. I had read so often, and seen so many pictures of this great defile in the northern landscape. Since I was a child I longed to go there and roam along the Whin Sill ledges that horseshoe above mighty precipices. High Cup Nick is a symbol of the wild and untamed nature of the northern hills, a massive gash that makes any wandering humans seem irrelevant in scale.

This incredible place is very familiar to anyone who has walked the higher stretches of the Pennine Way, for the oldest of our National Trails turns westward by the Nick and makes the long descent to the village of Dufton. To approach High Cup Nick in such a way, after miles of moorland walking, must be quite an experience, like tumbling of the edge of the world.

There was still snow on the Pennines' highest summit, Cross Fell, as I walked out from Dufton in a circuitous route that would take me to High Cup Nick from the south. The day did not bode well, for I felt ill, out of sorts, with a complete lack of energy. Every step was a trial, I felt breathless and my legs ached. There was no apparent reason for this lethargy that had beset me, only a feeling of general depression with life. They say that walking is a good cure for such melancholy moods. I have often found it so, particularly if the walk has some great scenic object that can only be reached with hard endeavour.

I was minded of the words of W.H. Davies, poet and super tramp, who thought lack of energy on walks might be just a state of mind. "The difference", he wrote, "between a good walker and a bad one, is that one walks with his heart and the other with his feet. As long as the heart is eager and willing, the strain on the body is not very important…no one should go forth as a wanderer unless he is a true love of Nature; for it is the ever-changing scenery that keeps his heart light until the end of the day's walk". Or as Shakespeare put it, succinctly, "Jog on, jog, on the footpath way, and merrily hent the stile-a, your merry heart goes all the way, your sad tires in a mile-a".

Certainly, I was cheered by the woodland scenery of Dufton Gill Wood, its St Bees sandstone rocks exposed for all to see in this landscape of wild and very visible geology. As I walked across farmland to Keisley Bridge, I remained on low ground, the great ridge of the Pennines to the east. This is the land of the Helm, that great stormy wind that can sweep without mercy down into the vale from the neighbouring hills. I have never witnessed it, but it is reported to be one of those terrible manifestations of nature that are never forgotten, once experienced. William Wordsworth's friend Thomas Wilkinson described it thus, in his 1824 book *Tours to the British Mountains:*

An assemblage of pale clouds extends to the summit of the mountain (Cross Fell); and, when all is calm on the plains, a roaring like the sea is heard to a considerable distance. I was once involved in the Helm Winds:- if I advanced it was with my head inclined to the ground, and at a slow pace; if I retreated and leaned against it with all my might, I could hardly keep erect; if I did not resist it I was blown over. A wind from the east rushed down the mountain with incredible fury: it broke the boughs from the trees, and tore the thatch from cottages at Melmerby and Gamblesby. But when I left this elemental tumult about two miles, all was perfectly calm, and a little further a gentle breeze sprang up from the West, while behind me the Helm Winds continued raging with unabated fury. Having heard uproars among mankind, and uproars among the elements, I prefer the latter, as having more sublimity.

I sat for a while on the parapet of the bridge over the Keisley Beck. Back out in the wild with nobody in sight, the last of my depression ebbed away. My muscles ceased to ache and my breathing became easier. This was better. This was what the roaming life was really all about. Just one individual in the heart of wild nature. My heart was merry, and I could have danced over the stile before me. It was a weekday and this was a holiday. I considered the millions in work that very same day, perhaps doing jobs that were an anathema to them, maybe for poor pay. I have done such work myself, dreading the lightening of the morning when I had to set out for another day's wage slavery. What right had I to be depressed? I had the freedom of the hills to look forward to, the hours were my own and I could go wherever I wanted to. Shackles loosened, I made my way passed a farm with the odd name of Harbour Flatt and then out on to the open fells.

This is wonderfully untamed country, where the Pennines drop so suddenly to the flood plains of the River Eden. Such a contrast of lands too, the wild moorland set against the flatter lands of wood and meadow. The track I followed led out on to the slopes of a very rocky hill called Middletongue, high above the tumbling waters of Trundale Gill, itself in as spectacular a valley as any fellwalker might wish for.

I climbed higher and higher, I found myself in the midst of wild and exposed moorland, broken up with patches of whin sill rock and hundreds of shake holes, a land shattered by the forces of geology. As I paused I could see the cultivated fields of Eden spread out from horizon to horizon, north to south, whilst before me were mile after mile of lonely fell. Skylarks hovered and danced overhead, and everywhere were the mournful cries of curlew and snipe.

I took my own line over Middletongue to the southern rim of High Cup Nick, where I stood in silence, bewildered by the incredible sight before me.

Descriptions and photographs do not do justice to High Cup Nick. In all my long years of walking I had never seen anything quite like it. This great gash in the Pennines almost defines the words, awesome, forbidding, magnificent. It is a deep canyon, boxed with mighty cliffs at one end, bar a narrow cut where the waters of High Cupgill Beck tumble through and down, the wind from the west blowing its spray back over the lip of the fall towards the moorland above. An overhanging lip of whin sill lines the edges of the great valley, huge slopes of grey scree climbing up to meet it, these cliffs broken by the white lines of waterfalls, tiny becks achieving majesty as they tumble hundreds of feet to join the river far below.

I have never had much fear of heights, but there was that about High Cup Nick that made me want to sit down lest I succumbed to the maniac urge to roll over that exposed cliff edge. High Cup Nick seems like one of those places in legend where quests are resolved, where heroes engage in final battles, and where the mighty come to die.

I wandered around the southern rim to the waterfall itself, finding quite a tiny beck flowing in from the gentle slope of the fells. I scrambled a little way down the waterfall to get the best view down the valley, the westerly wind blowing the odd spume across my back, cooling in the hot weather.

The thought occurred to me that this must be a terrible place when the Helm Wind is at its fiercest. I followed the route of the Pennine Way around the Nick's northern edge and clambered out on to the rocky crag known as Nichol's Chair, supposedly named after a Dufton cobbler who sat there and mended some shoes. It was a precarious perch for me just sitting still, the great drop below reminding me that I was not immortal. But it was a wonderful place to be, my earlier depression vanquished with the sheer joy of living. I remembered the schoolteacher who branded me 'challenge dependent' at quite an early age. Perhaps he was right.

I pulled back a short distance to eat lunch on the edge of the Pennine Way, waving a greeting at a party of quite elderly ramblers who came by, heading for the head of the waterfall. I watched as they reached there and then they disappeared down into the chasm. I thought that they had probably just halted for lunch, but the sounds of exhilarated yelling from the party took me back to the edge. There they were, scrambling down the boulder field beside the waterfall and evidently enjoying every minute of the experience. Now, I had glimpsed them on the way up the track and the youngest must have been way over seventy. I was filled with admiration. I felt ashamed at my earlier bemoaning of aches and pains. I watched as they reached the bottom of the cliff, and smiled at their great shout of triumph.

I headed down the Pennine Way back to Dufton, stopping every few yards to gain yet a different view of High Cup Nick and, in the other direction, a vista of the familiar mountains of the Lake District. As I turned a corner in the track, High Cup Nick was lost from view, and I plodded into Dufton, where I sat for a while on the green, reminiscing about the day's walk.

I like Dufton, the village of the Doves, its cottages lining a pleasant green, with the fells still in sight. W.H. Auden thought it the prettiest village in England. Its Post Office opened then on Sunday teatimes to cater for the walkers coming down from the hills. I ordered tea and a sandwich and sat outside. I was joined after a while by the husband of the proprietor. Asking if he was local, he replied that he was from Birmingham, and we reminisced for a while about many Black Country localities. He spoke of the ferocity of the Helm Wind, and recalled a Chihuahua dog he had once had who had been a superb navigator on the Pennine fells.

A few days later, I was in Bowness-on-Windermere and strolled into a place selling antiquarian books and prints, for old books about the countryside are a passion for me. There was nothing I wanted in the book line, but among the framed prints I found an old engraving of High Cup Nick. It adorns my wall to this day and I cannot pass it without recalling the moody atmosphere of that great cleft in the western edge of the Pennines.

~

I've always liked the little town of Kirkby Stephen, an unpretentious halting point on the Coast to Coast Walk from St Bees Head to Robin Hood's Bay, a tremendous long distance walk devised by the greatest of all fellwalkers, Alfred Wainwright. The town itself is without airs, a long street leading to an old market square where goods have been sold since its market charter was granted in 1361. Its large church is even older, boasting some wonderful ancient tombs, and displaying a carved cross, sacred to the Norse god Loki, which is well over a thousand years old. The centre of Kirkby Stephen is a busy place, filled with people coming and going; farmers' landrovers, and hikers following in Wainwright's footsteps. There is a friendliness about the people in these parts; they stop for a chat, and serve you with a smile in the local shops.

I saw the Nine Standards at a distance on my first visit to Kirkby Stephen, strange standing objects on the long Pennine ridge, several miles west of the town. I didn't know what they were but soon found out. Nine Standards Rigg, the Ordnance Survey map calls them. Tall cairns atop the hill, like old grey men keeping a weary watch.

One of the legends about the Nine Standards is that they were built to convince raiding Scots that a deterring army was encamped upon the hill. A simpler explanation is that the Nine Standards are boundary stones. Whatever the reason for their construction, they are massive and can be seen from miles away in all directions.

On a beautifully clear April morning I sat on a bench close by Frank's Bridge, below the town, preparing to walk up the long hill to the Nine Standards. The very narrow Frank's Bridge crosses the River Eden on the line of an ancient lich way into the town, the route by which corpses were transported to the church in Kirkby Stephen. Today it seems to be where the residents of the town come to relax, to sit by the river and feed the ducks. It is certainly a very pleasant place to linger, and it took some effort to tear myself away and head for the hills, or more immediately the attractive village of Hartley, a mile away from the town.

It was in the trees just before Hartley that I first encountered the parrots. The three birds looked down from a branch and chattered away to me. As I walked on, they followed, full of conversation. As I explored Hartley, they dogged my footsteps. A villager explained that a Kirkby resident kept a great many parrots, parakeets and macaws, and that they all flew free during the day, returning to their aviaries to be fed and at night. They certainly brought a touch of the tropical to my walk, soaring ahead of me from tree to tree. The birds seemed quiet and attentive when I talked to them, but shrieked with annoyance when I broke off the conversation and walked on. As I left the village up the appropriately named Fell Lane, they gave up on me and flew in formation back towards Kirkby.

I followed the lane as it curved round a massive and unsightly aggregates quarry and headed steeply uphill to become a charming and unfenced country lane. In the distance stretched the snow-covered summit of Wild Boar Fell, where Sir Richard Musgrave supposedly slaughtered the last wild boar in these parts. There may be some truth in this legend, for when his tomb in Kirkby Stephen church was opened in the nineteenth century two tusks were found with his body. They may be seen in a small exhibition case in that building to this day.

Fell Lane petered out on the north west edge of Hartley Fell, becoming a rough track. Every now and again I would get glimpses of the Nine Standards, sometimes seeming to be very near and then farther away, in the usual habit of summits, where you feel that you are about to arrive, only to be thwarted by another climbing mile. At one point a couple of guiding cairns by the side of the track created the optical illusion of *being* the Standards, only to thwart me as I came abreast of them. I was on the open fell side by now, heading directly towards the Nine Standards by the side of a tumbling beck called Faraday Gill.

The first real sight of the Nine Standards makes the long uphill from Kirkby Stephen well worthwhile. The cairns are magnificent, huge stone giants strung almost in a line along the hillside. There is something almost forbidding about their presence which dominates the edge of such lonely moorland. As I wandered there, I considered why they were built? I can well believe that this spectacle might deter some passing invader; the cairns have that air about them. I certainly do not accept the theory that they were erected as boundary stones. Why build so many? And the boundary of what? No one has ever dated the

Nine Standards. They could be prehistoric, but are probably of much later date.

Whatever, they are bold and mysterious, standing like old grey men on the border between the cultivated valley of the Eden and the remote stretches of this northern wilderness.

One point is not in dispute. The Nine Standards can be seen for miles around, and the view from them takes your breath away. To the highest Pennine height of Cross Fell to the north, and across to the Lakeland fells and the dales of Yorkshire.

As I walked around the moorland, grouse took to the sky, muttering cries of annoyance, and skylarks, hardly visible, hovered and sung. It is hard to grasp the scale of this great wilderness, one of the remotest areas of Britain. I stood at the highest point of the fell, by a direction indicator placed by the local fell rescue group to commemorate the wedding of Prince Charles and Lady Diana Spencer in 1981, and contemplated that this great desert would take a lifetime to know. There is such a feeling of space amidst such moorland, a rarity in our overcrowded island. I felt high, and had a wonderful energy, as though I were breathing extra oxygen.

Nine Standards Rigg is a hard place to leave behind, and I reluctantly turned downhill to Kirkby Stephen. As I descended my mind drifted into the old times of this place, when fire and blood were the indicators of conflict in this remote region. I looked across the valley beyond the little town of Brough to Stainmore, where the Viking king Eric Bloodaxe was ambushed and slain. There were terrible times in this now peaceful landscape. Perhaps the old stone men of Nine Standards mark the site of some long-forgotten battle? They are certainly a symbol of these very wild Pennines.

"Are you the winner?" an old gentlemen asked as I crossed Frank's Bridge, mistaking me for a member of an organised run. "No," I replied. "Just a survivor." And as I climbed the lane into the town that is what I seemed to be, somehow different to the crowds who had not been up to the Nine Standards that day. From the boundary of the town I looked back up the hillside and caught a glimpse of the glowering giants, and felt that I had encountered something not quite of this world.

~

Like the poet Edward Thomas, I don't mind walking in the rain, whether in the mountains or across lowland pastures. On a very wet spring day I arrived in Appleby to explore the lovely countryside by the River Eden.

Appleby is best known as the setting for a famous horse fair, when Gypsies and travellers arrive from all over Britain to buy and sell horses, tell fortunes, and snatch a few moments of a journeying way of life that is now no more. There were no Gypsies in sight as I wandered up the main street towards the castle, under threatening skies.

Appleby was once the county town of Westmorland, until sad and unimaginative bureaucrats erased that ancient county from the map. Not that you would know that on the ground, for the spirited folk of the district have maintained their "Welcome to Westmorland" signs at the old county boundaries, and few ever talk of Appleby being in Cumbria. To keep its old county town traditions alive, the town of Appleby changed its name to Appleby-in-Westmorland.

Westmorland is surely one of the most beautiful words in our language. Let us hope it is not too long before the hideous catch-all of Cumbria is despatched into obscurity, and these wild regions restored to the old counties of Westmorland, Cumberland and Lancashire.

Appleby's castle is shut to the public most of the time because of some squabble between its owners and English Heritage - a pity, because its buildings are a fine sight, high above the River Eden. As I looked at it through the castle gate the rain began to speckle down, and by the time I was on the banks of the Eden it was pouring, bouncing and dancing on the surface of the river.

Walking the meadows by the Eden is very pleasant, even in wet weather. The right of way is a real poacher's path, sometimes running across open fields, then through the woodlands that edge down to the course of the river. The pastures were crammed with sheep, the ewes moving their many lambs uphill and out of my range before following me from stile to stile, making a terrific noise as they went. I posited the idea that they had been trained thus by the local river board to draw attention to illicit fishermen. Only in the woods would any poacher be free from observation.

By now the rain was pelting down, and I sought shelter in a walking cape. My walking cape is almost a portable tent that pulls over my entire body, head, rucksack and all, leaving exposed just the lower half of the legs. It can only be used on lowland walks as it catches the wind too much on higher ground. The cape is very effective; you really feel that you are shut off from the worst elements of the weather. I loathe waterproofs generally, finding them clammy and, after a while, ineffective. There have been days when I have been thoroughly soaked thanks to a reluctance to wear the wretched things. But on days of persistent rain I usually start with one on.

Yet despite the weather I felt free and happy and considered that every day not spent afoot was a day wasted. The tune of the *Wraggle Taggle Gypsies* ran persistently through my head and I sang and whistled its infernal melody out loud. I waved my walking staff in the air. I leaped from the stiles and yelled with joy, startling a pair of herons who flapped across to the far bank to get away from me. I sheltered for a moment or two under a railway viaduct of the Settle to Carlisle line, and then walked into the tiny village of Great Ormside.

Now Orm was a Viking, probably one of the Halfdans who raided and pillaged the kingdom of Northumbria and then settled in these parts. The church and the Pele Tower in the neighbouring farm shows that defence was a priority for the people who farmed this valley, both in Viking times and in the centuries when the Scots invaded the area. The old church is mostly Norman but built high on a defensive mound, which started out as a pagan burial ground.

It was here that the Ormside Bowl was found in 1823, probably a Saxon relic looted by the Viking inhabitants of this place. Standing by the church door I could imagine how the people of Ormside might seek refuge in the church during troublous times. The old building could well survive a short siege and, with the nearby Pele Tower, might deter Scottish warriors who would seek easier prey. It was on an expedition to quell the might of Scotland that the Black Prince, that martial son and heir to Edward III, passed this way in 1376. Feeling unwell he made his will at Great Ormside, courtesy of the church's priest John de Grote. He died soon afterwards, before completing his journey north. Such are the ways that the greater history of England touches the most seemingly forgotten places.

Certainly, the world seems to have passed by Great Ormside. The public house seemed to be shut up as I walked up the village street, but a Gypsy wagon added colour to the scene. Railway trains run by the village, but the station is now a private home. Just beyond was a place for new age retreat, called "Dancing Bear", offering 'alternative accommodation' in yurts, sweat lodges and saunas, and offering 'drumming workshops'. There seemed to be no one about so I walked out of the village to an isolated cottage with the intriguing name of 'Donkey's Nest' called more prosaically 'Porch Cottage' on the Ordnance Survey map, from which a muddy footpath took me over to Rutter Force.

There are some places in Britain that picture postcards might have been invented for, and the waterfall of Rutter Force is one, with its accompanying mill building and waterwheel, a couple of attractive cottages, a ford, and a rustic bridge. I had seen it before in pictures. Indeed, every shop in the district sells pictures, cards and prints of this idyllic scene.

Even in the pouring rain it looked pretty, and I leaned against the bridge and admired its crashing waters for several minutes. One of the cottages was a teashop come art gallery and flinging off my cape I went inside. I was the only customer but was made very welcome by the proprietor and his waitress, who brought me tea and toast, and kept refilling the teapot as we chatted about the weather and local places to visit. I have seldom had such a warm welcome, and I was reluctant to head back out into the storm. Sadly, the cafe has now gone.

Later at Bandley Bridge sipping tea, and staring out from my hood at the still pouring rain. But all the birds of spring were still singing in this very peaceful countryside.

It was just a stroll back into Appleby from the Bridge, the rain easing a little as it tends to do just as you are finishing a walk.

Some months later I did again the walk to Rutter Force and the Hoff Beck, this time in the baking heat of one of the hottest summers on record. As I ascended the hill from Bandley Bridge I came upon the local farmer and his wife gathering in the harvest from the great field atop the ridge, their harvesters laying out great rolls of hay, for all the world like chickens laying eggs. Some way up the field were the farming couple by their landrover.

We talked, as farmers and walkers so often do when they come together, of the weather, the great blaze of sun and drought that had beset the land for months. I told them of my walk in the rain, not so long before, as we all eyed a sky of unbroken blue.

Sitting in a café in Appleby I reflected on this walk under the brow of the high Pennines, and made notes on my wet day in Eden, the beautiful little church at Great Ormside, the warm welcome I had received at Rutter Force, and the quiet pastures around the Hoff Beck.

Sometimes, in reflective mood, I sit at home and look back on these walks and find it hard to believe that there are such places in what so often seems overcrowded England.

As I sipped my cup of tea that day in Appleby, a horse drawn Gypsy wagon crossed the old bridge and took the road leading to the wilder country of the north Pennines, a sight that gladdened my heart, being so far removed from the terrors of twenty-first century life and all that makes the modern world something that you wish to escape from.

I picked up my rucksack and headed once more to the outdoors.

Solitary

To gain the most from a period of vagabondage you really need to walk alone. This isn't to say that walking in company totally destroys the atmosphere of a good walk. There are times when we all crave companionship, and I've enjoyed walking with certain individuals over the years, and have learned a lot from the people I've journeyed with. But I'm not by nature a group walker, though I've led numerous rambling parties. Robert Louis Stevenson hit the nail on the head in his marvellous essay 'Walking Tours' when he writes:

> *Now, to be properly enjoyed, a walking tour should be gone on alone. If you go in a company, or even in pairs, it is no longer a walking tour in anything but name; it is something else and more in the nature of a picnic. A walking tour should be gone on alone, because freedom is of the essence; because you should be able to stop and go on, and follow this way or that, as the freak takes you; and because you must have your own pace... And then you must be open to all impressions and let your thoughts take colour from what you see. You should be as the pipe for any wind to play upon. "I cannot see the wit," says Hazlitt, "of walking and talking at the same time. When I am in the country I wish to vegetate like the country,"- which is the gist of all that can be said upon the matter. There should be no cackle of voices at your elbow, to jar on the meditative silence of the morning. And so long as a man is reasoning he cannot surrender himself to that fine intoxication that comes of so much motion in the open air, that begins in a sort of dazzle and sluggishness of the brain, and ends in a peace that passes comprehension.*

You might argue that, of course, writers need to walk alone to gain material for their work, to be able to give impressions of people and places uninterrupted by other parties. Artists who need to lose themselves in the peace and quiet of the countryside, unhindered by the presence of anyone else. As the great pre-war tramper A.J. Brown remarked, "to walk in company is prose, to walk alone is poetry".

When you walk alone the 'mind cinema', as that great walker John Hillaby described it comes into play. You soak up the atmosphere of the places you pass through both consciously and subconsciously. Your mind drifts into other scenarios, oblivious to the tread of your feet. Walking becomes a kind of moving meditation in which you seem to live several lives, as random thoughts dash across your mind. You can talk to yourself, either aloud or in your head, compose speeches, sing songs, ward off imaginary foes.

The best of your thoughts can be put into your notebook during your rest stops. You can make an artist of yourself. The halts are every bit as important and satisfying when you walk alone. You can hold your journey for as little or long a time as you choose, cherishing the hour spent on the mountain summit, or the time dozing and thinking, your back resting against a downland tumulus, as you consider the meaning of life.

You can talk to the people you encounter on your adventure. Strangers feel less inhibited when they hold conversation with one person, more inclined to talk and tell you of the wonders of their district.

The great writers of the past, George Borrow, Edward Thomas, Stephen Graham, gained a surfeit of stories by walking alone, having the freedom to listen intently at such encounters and being able to memorise and record without interruption. Jean-Jacques Rousseau remarked that "never did I think so much, exist so vividly and experience so much, as in the journeys I have taken alone and on foot".

Some people, naturally, frown on solitary roaming, especially in the mountains, where accidents can happen. Lone mountain walking comes in for a great deal of criticism. Anxious friends posit the possibility that you might be taken ill and be helpless, that you might break an ankle or leg, and die of exposure, no one knowing exactly where you are.

Sensible books on walking tell you to leave word of where you are going with some responsible person, or even on a note pinned to your car. Some even tell you never to walk alone, lest you have a fall. Now it is true, all of these dire events *might* happen. The world is an unsafe place and the human body is pretty vulnerable to mishap.

But for the outdoor man such injunctions are a positive anathema. Experienced hillwalkers tend not to stick absolutely to the route they intended to follow when they set out that morning. They are too often lured by the temptations of a different summit, or the promise of the ridge beyond. They may set out to walk from village to village, but get sidetracked by the sunny banks of a beautiful tarn, or need the freedom to roam in every sense of that expression, free of the constrictions and nannying of an over-protective society. One day a walker might tumble and break a bone or have a heart attack, but so might we all in any environment.

Walking across the hills or through the depths of the countryside is often safer and usually a great deal more pleasant than negotiating the back streets of some of our cities. This is not to suggest that you should not take sensible precautions. You need to bear in mind the possibility of an accident or illness, carry sufficient supplies and be adequately equipped. You should know how to use a map and compass and recognise escape routes if you feel unwell or if the weather closes in.

If you lack experience or confidence then perhaps you should leave word of where you are going, but only if you are absolutely sure that you will stick to that planned route. If you are a complete novice, particularly in the sphere of mountain walking, then it might be a good idea to begin your adventures in the company of experienced friends in a rambling club. But if you do then offer to lead sometimes, so that you might build up that well of experience that will allow you to tackle the heights on your own.

Some people never walk alone and get a great amount of pleasure from their adventures with other people and in the casual conversations of rambling friends. But I feel that they miss out on a great deal; the quiet of the summer meadows, the exhilaration of attaining a mighty summit at your own pace, the reflective thoughts as you head home in the twilight after a long and satisfying day in the hills.

Such solitary wanderings build a host of memories for old age when roving might be beyond your physical capabilities. Life is short. Make the most of every precious moment. But if you do find the ideal walking companion, do feel free to throw all of these solitary recommendations aside.

Lakeland

Every visitor to the Kirkstone Pass and its famous inn is familiar with Red Screes, the precipitous height towering above the car park. Climbing Red Screes feels very much like playing to the gallery - all the time you climb you are being watched by at least some spectators, and the glint of binoculars below could give the nervous fell wanderer stage fright. Like most Lake District mountains, there are easier ways up than the direct route from Kirkstone, but none gives the satisfaction than does that scrambling ascent.

On a full stomach, from a wonderful Lakeland breakfast, the first hundred yards of grass seemed heavy going and very steep. But having spent weeks hillwalking in the Scottish Highlands I was very fit and soon began to feel muscles start to work and breathing ease. This was my first ascent of Red Screes. I have climbed it since, but no occasion has been as memorable as the first.

After the steep grass, the rock and scree begins. Red Screes is well named, particularly when seen by motorists on the way up from Troutbeck. The scree is indeed of the deepest red, as though an artist had drawn his brush with that colour all the way down the rocky coves of the mountain. On this bright June day, the red glowed and dazzled in the morning sunshine.

It always surprises me in hill country how quickly you seem to make height. I had not been climbing for very long before the cars and people in the pass below seemed ridiculously miniature; the people rather like full stops and their vehicles mere blobs of colour, and then not even that. The white inn transformed into something resembling the houses you get as an accessory for a model railway. The Kirkstone is a very handy pub, I considered.

A fall in the right direction and a considerable bit of outward drift, and you could literally drop in for a drink.

By now the rock had become so steep that I put away the trekking poles on to the rucksack, so that I might have my hands free for the endeavour. Much of the ascent is running scree, with bits of solid rock in between. Both hands are needed to secure yourself as you climb. High above was the gap in the rock that I knew led to Kilnshaw Chimney, the way out on to the summit of the mountain. I wandered how hard that last bit was going to be? I sat on a rock that hung perilously over the incline for a swig of water, feeling terribly thirsty and suspecting that stopping places might be hard to come by as I went on. The cars and people in the pass were now barely identifiable, so far were they below. The way I had come seemed incredibly sheer to me as I looked down.

But then I began to enjoy the exposure. Adventure is, after all, a calculated risk. It was good to be there, far away and above the usual sedentary and boring world. This was living, and as I climbed every thought that might beleaguer my mind and bring me down in the workaday world had gone, there remained just the concentrative need to spy out a possible path to the top. Occasionally a foot would rest on a stone that would suddenly move, so I became careful what I was balancing my weight upon.

The June morning sun was hot and lit up the cliffside, beating down upon me with all its summer's worth, bringing on a thirst and sweating out the moisture. But even on such a still dry day there was the constant sound of water drip-drip-dripping down the rock face. The stones that I gripped were increasingly wet and slippery.

Near to the top of a line of crags, I chose a route going off to the left. The chimney was quite narrow with some very steep stretches. At one point a glance showed a drop of a hundred feet or more down into the gully, which would leave the unlucky climber who fell, injured or possibly dead high on the side of the mountain. Not a terrifically good place to fall off, I decided. I squirmed upwards into the narrowing chimney, then putting my feet on the rocks to one side I climbed out on to an earthy slope, very wet with stony cliffs to each side. At first I put the wrong foot on a foothold and felt myself going off balance. I swore with annoyance, for this meant a delicate lowering movement to get the next foot in place. I reached out and hauled myself on to the grassy slope above.

From there it was an easy couple of hundred yards' stroll to the summit cairn - or rather cairns, for there are several. I lay down on the grass and poured liquid into me, as the midday sun beat down.

All the drama of Red Screes is on its eastern slopes above the Kirkstone Pass. To the west the mountain is a long rolling moorland hill, though with extensive views over Coniston Old Man, Wetherlam, Scafell and Great Gable - those great mountains of Lakeland. I looked to the east from the shores of Windermere to the western heights of the Kentmere Horseshoe. As I admired the views and took lunch, several fell walkers came up to the summit, all from the easier direction of Ambleside, rather than up Kilnshaw Chimney from Kirkstone.

It was becoming crowded, so I headed northwards, descending slightly, to the summit of Middle Dodd, in effect a spur and secondary of the great ridge of which Red Screes is the central portion. The distance between the two tops is scarcely a mile, but the views that are revealed over the little lake of Brothers Water are staggeringly beautiful. As I sat on rocks at the end of the spur, watching the cloud shadows dance over Dove

Crag, I thought of the rock climbers of earlier times, such as Don Whillans, who had put up many routes in the neighbourhood, the easiest far harder than my modest little scramble. Still, it was enough for me.

As the sun broke through the crags became clear, the sunlight delineating every crack and gully. Helvellyn loomed up to meet the clouds and I could hear the crash of water from the waterfalls of the Caiston Beck a thousand feet below. All around were summits, and a distant glimpse of Ullswater. It was a classic Lakeland view that turned my heart over as I looked around.

Suddenly summer vanished as a harsh and cold wind struck the hill. Great Gable was lost into thick, dark cloud. As I strolled back up to the summit of Red Screes, Helvellyn disappeared and a great band of cloud rolled in overhead. As I reached the summit cairn which offered some rough shelter, the rain began to sweep in sideways across the ridge. Tiny isolated clouds scat up the Kirkstone valley level with the summit. The fell walkers remaining on the summit fled for low ground in the direction of Ambleside, like so many minnows chased by a pike, but I decided to sit out the storm in the lee of the cairn, sipping tea and eating chocolate.

In moments the clouds lowered and the top was engulfed in mist, moving quickly in and out in the sudden and gusty wind. Although it was June, the rain turned to sleet, then - for a few minutes - snow, for mountains make their own weather whatever the season of the year, before turning back to rain.

Every now and again almost perfectly square windows of visibility appeared in the cloud atop the valley, giving glimpses of the rugged heights of Ill Bell and Froswick standing proud in brilliant sunshine, like stage sets illuminated by limelight.

The remaining walkers on the summit head down as the cloud lifts for a moment - a mother, father and child. The parents had smoked and looked anxious as the weather closed in, but the child seemed more interested in the teddy bear she carried in her tiny rucksack. They disappeared from view as the cloud skirted above them as they hurried from the top.

Eventually the wind eased off and I contemplated my own descent. All day I had been kidding myself that I would take the gentler route to Ambleside, before cutting across to the lane up towards the Kirkstone Pass, but I had known in my heart that I would seek a more direct and steeper way down.

And down I went into a murderously slippery chimney that led onto the steep and rocky combe on the south-eastern corner of the mountain. As I gingerly threaded my way down moving scree, I glanced up to see two walkers up by Raven Crag, watching me with disbelief. Well, that was just an impression for I could not see their faces.

Each step I took went several inches further than I intended as the mountain scree moved beneath me. In such conditions it is important to keep as upright as possible. Once you go off balance you are lost. The red scree was wringing wet, which didn't help and all around tiny runnels of water were being transformed into little waterfalls as the rain swept across this great bowl in the mountain. Foot muscles ached as they bent at such a peculiar angle to maintain friction with the wet surface of the mountain. Until - at last - I was on leveller ground.

A rocky path threaded back through grassy slopes and tiny crags to the Kirkstone Pass. The car park was full now, as tourists slept off their Sunday lunches or looked up with mixed interest at the crags. A hundred yards more and I am with them and one of them, looking up to the mist-shrouded mountain. As

I leaned against a wall I looked up Red Screes and found it hard to believe that I had been more than a spectator.

~

I've always had a fascination for mountain passes. Perhaps it is being able to picture those who journeyed the hill tracks in times gone by, or just the drama of the mountain scenery.

I liked the name Nan Bield the first time I encountered it, in one of William Palmer's books about Lakeland. Palmer is a neglected figure these days, his many volumes about walking gathering dust in antiquarian bookshops, to be taken down and purchased by the more discerning fell walkers. His work was popular long before Alfred Wainwright began his detailed exploration of the Lakeland fells.

Palmer was a true mountain man, born close to Kendal, an editor of the *Journal* of the Fell and Rock climbing club, and a voluminous author about most of the hill districts of Britain.

The Nan Bield Pass lies at the head of the near circuit of mountains known to fell walkers as the Kentmere Horseshoe. It is true to say that it is on this great walk than most walkers now encounter Nan Bield; fewer walk the line of the ancient pass leading from the Kentmere Valley to Mardale. I decided to have the best of both worlds. I would walk the ridges high above the valley and walk back to Kentmere along the ancient trackway from Nan Bield. This gave me the opportunity to climb the Garburn Pass, the old route from Kentmere to Troutbeck, as well.

I'm glad I did, for the Garburn Pass has a real mountain feel to it, winding upwards in zigzags and very rocky both underfoot and all around. I could imagine the drovers of old forcing their sheep and cattle upwards, and feeling a sigh of relief when the beautiful valley of Troutbeck came into view, when the moorland at the head of the pass was reached. The scenery on the climb is certainly spectacular, with wide views back over Kentmere and the slopes covered in boulders and rocky tors.

At the top of the pass I headed northwards towards the summit of the improbably named mountain Yoke. It was very easy going, a good track just inside a stone wall across moorland. As I gained height, views opened up towards Troutbeck and much of the entire length of Lake Windermere. The summit of Yoke is not particularly spectacular, just a couple of small cairns, but the scenery all around is wonderful, particularly towards Helvellyn. The ridge narrowed at Star Crag, revealing a craggy drop down to the little Kentmere Reservoir, with its surrounding quarries, and the great precipice of Ill Bell.

It is at this latter mountain that the ridge becomes truly mountainous, with steep slopes into the Kentmere valley on one side and the vale above Troutbeck on the other. I had felt myself unfit on the climb up the Garburn Pass, but now I had plenty of energy to spare. There is something about ridge walking where you top several summits that does this. It is as though the narrowing earth pours a force into you that replenishes any depleted strength.

From a distance Froswick, the next summit on the ridge, looks like a mirror image of Ill Bell, one of those perfect dual creations that gives a feeling that there is some deliberate artistry in nature. I lay for a while on its top and admired the surrounding views of Lakeland and the distant Pennines. I had intended to cut round to Nan Bield from this point, but a surfeit of energy bade me include the summits of Thornthwaite Crag and High Street in my journey.

Thornthwaite is certainly no crag in reality, but that misrepresentation is more than made up for by the magnificent pillar cairn, mounted in the corner of a drystone on its highest point - perhaps one of the best cairns in all Lakeland. I sat there for a while and considered the weather. Although it was still clear and I could see back to Windermere in the south and over to Fairfield and Helvellyn to the west, there was a kind of iron band of haze a few hundred feet overhead.

There was not a hint of wind and only the skylarks and sheep broke the mountain silence. It felt like the lull before a storm, one of those occasions in the hills where the earth seems mighty and the individual human being tiny and insignificant. I considered heading straight for Nan Bield and back into the valley, but I had never visited High Street and thought I would have time.

I was glad I did, as it turned out there was no storm that day; the lull was one of nature's false alarms. I walked on to the great massif of High Street. The approach offered sensational views over a craggy edge with the tiny lake of Hayes Water far below. So bewitched was I by this ruggedness that I almost forgot to steer off for High Street's summit. Not that there is much to see at the top of this most venerable of Lake District fells; one battered wall, a redundant Ordnance Survey triangulation pillar, and a couple of low cairns. But think of all the history!

High Street takes its name from the road built by the Romans across the broad top of this mountain some two thousand years ago. Legions marched this way between the garrisons of Ambleside and Brougham. In recent centuries the folk of the dales held great feasts here, racing horses across its acres of heather. Until recently, it was still called Racecourse Hill.

As I sat on the summit I could see the colour and hear the noise of the crowds. But now the colour was the dun of the hill and the sounds were those of grazing animals and circling birds. No other human was in sight, the sixty millions of these islands were elsewhere. For an hour or two High Street was mine.

It was late afternoon before I could tear myself away, a tad tired now, but the tiredness of physical satisfaction. I made my way down to the rather confused summit of Mardale Ill Bell, no relation to the earlier summit of this walk. Presumably the folk of Mardale wanted an Ill Bell all of their own. This was a broken and very rocky landscape and, in one of its depressions, no more than a mountain col, is the narrow track of the Nan Bield Pass. In the dip of the pass is a three-walled shelter, built presumably to give some cover to any traveller caught out by nightfall or bad weather, Bield being a Lakeland term for a hide or shelter.

That grand fell walk the Kentmere Horseshoe climbs away here on to Harter Fell and then Kentmere Pike. I was sorely tempted to continue, but I really wanted to experience some of the journey travellers would have taken through the Nan Bield Pass. The path was narrow and steep and zigzagged wildly down the side of the mountain into the sanctuary at the head of the Kentmere valley. It was astonishingly beautiful in the early evening light, a mixture of brown and grey ruggedness, contrasted with the green of the lower vale.

As the steepness ended, a long path contoured the hillside above the Kentmere reservoir. All around were signs that man has worked the hillside, from the grey quarries to the drystone walls. I sat on a boulder and watched as a couple of shepherds and half a dozen barking dogs rounded up and sorted a flock of Herdwick sheep, moving some into a lower pasture and releasing others out on to the hillside. I appreciated the stop as tiredness was setting in. It seemed to be one of those paths that go on for ever, destination never being reached. The evening was hot, I was thirsty, and Kentmere seemed to be always just below.

A broad bridleway by Overend Farm, shady and cool after the heat on the open fells, brought me back to the tiny village. It turned out that I had been lucky with the weather on the tops; it had rained in Windermere for much of the day.

As I fell into a dreamless sleep back in Staveley, the rain bucketed down. Apart from visiting the head of two mountain passes, I had been over six summits. That journey has always stayed in my mind and the Nan Bield Pass become a vision of the best of mountain scenery.

~

While it is always wonderful to ascend the higher mountains of Britain, particularly those over 3000 feet, such as the Munros in Scotland, I never judge a mountain by its height. The attraction might be the mountain's shape, the drama of its position, or just the way you feel about it on the day.

I had always liked the look of Stone Arthur, that rocky tor so visible from the streets of Grasmere. In point of fact, Stone Arthur is not even a major peak, just a subsidiary summit on the ridge coming down from the greater top of Great Rigg.

I enjoy walking from Grasmere. It's a true mountain village, surrounded by tantalising high ground. In every direction is a wonderful mountain walk and the beauty of the scenery is hard to beat. Alfred Wainwright, the apostle of fellwalking, came to loathe the place, thinking it overrun with tourists. And so it often is, particularly on summer days when trippers throng around

Wordsworth's grave, Dove Cottage and its many and varied souvenir shops.

But scratch below the surface or visit on a quieter winter's day and the old Grasmere is still there, the lonely outpost that would have been so familiar to Wordsworth, Coleridge and De Quincy. Even for a discerning shopper it has wonderful advantages; Sam Read's is everything a traditional bookshop should be and more, a good place to browse after a hard day in the hills. There is another shop I like, an antique and curiosity shop that has a good selection of antiquarian books. Many of the titles on my own bookshelves have been purchased there, and each old book has become a memory in its way of the walk in the mountains that preceded or succeeded its buying. On the late September day that I climbed Stone Arthur, the book was a 1903 volume on the Lakeland Fells by the neglected local author William Palmer, a man who knew all of the mountains thereabouts like few authors. If I could not roam in Palmer's company, I could at least carry his book up into places that were special to him.

Torrential rain had lashed the mountains for the past couple of days and the sound of running water was everywhere. The storm had broken just before dawn and the last scattered shower clouds weaved around and across the mountain tops. I walked up from the Swan Hotel to the waterfall of Greenhead Gill, its tumultuous sounds crashing down towards the steep lane. The path out on to the open fells was carrying a great deal of water, almost a stream washing over my boots as I made for higher ground.

It felt a lengthier slog than it really was, but there were excellent views over the great bowl of Grasmere and the surrounding mountains, which brought back so many memories of long days on the fells. The mountains of so many yesterdays. As I watched, climbed summits would disappear into the clouds and as suddenly re-emerge. I could visualize their tops, the routes of ascent, the adventures I had had. I scarcely noticed my arrival at Stone Arthur, so filled was I with remembrances of other days.

I had lunch with my back to one of the great boulders of Stone Arthur, watching the clouds as they rolled across the valley. For a moment the higher peak of Seat Sandal loomed out of the cloud layer only to disappear.

I had fond memories of that neglected mountain. Only a year before I had sat against its summit cairn on a day of better visibility and heard a muffled conversation between two or three people not many yards away. There was no one in sight. As far as I could tell I was alone on the mountain. Were they the ghosts of some long past fell wanderers? Sounds do carry in strange ways in the mountains so perhaps not. Maybe the conversations echoed across the ether from a neighbouring peak. Maybe there really was a supernatural explanation. Sometimes in the mountains you do feel that you are on the boundary of some other world.

I was dwelling on that experience when someone said "hello" from close at hand. I looked up into the smiling face of a young man. He sat on a rock across from me and told me he was on holiday from Rickmansworth and had come up from Grasmere, heading out to Great Rigg. We talked for a while about the weather and other climbs, as you do, and then about fellwalking generally.

"I had a friend once" he told me, "he'd done a fair amount of fellwalking but very little actual climbing. He'd been dating this nurse, but she dumped him because she couldn't put up with his tramping. Anyway, he set off on a ferocious rock climb to 'forget'. Half way up, he fell off. He was lucky, just a broken ankle. By coincidence the rescue people rushed him to the hospital where his erstwhile love worked."

"And was she overcome with guilt?" I asked.

"Not likely! I think he expected to get a great burst of sympathy, but it didn't happen. She said he was a bloody fool and that he'd get no comfort from her!" Such are the ways of those who do not feel the desire to wander. I said farewell and journeyed on.

Now I had intended to have a lazy day and only climb as far as Stone Arthur. But Lakeland ridges are seductive and it was still very early, so I decided to walk awhile up the ridge towards Great Rigg. The clouds had gone and the sky was blue with all the neighbouring summits in view.

To the south the waters of Alcock Tarn shone like a bead of light from the mountainside. It is said that the word tarn is Viking for tear; so they look as the sun catches them, tears on the slopes of the mountains. As I walked on ravens swooped and kronked around my head.

But as I approached the Rigg, a huge bank of cloud swept in from the west, enveloping the mountainside. It reminded me of a couple of years before, when I'd walked this path in the opposite direction, finishing the Fairfield Horseshoe, and on just such a cloudy day. As I descended I witnessed an optical illusion. A great tunnel had appeared in the mist, through which had flooded silver light and then a very clear and magnified image of what were obviously the fells around Coniston. The view seemed to dangle in mid-air and appeared nearer than the ridge to either side of me. Instead of looking down or across to these distant fells I felt that I was looking up to them.

Such inexplicable events occur on mountain walks.

Great Rigg is hardly noticeable as a top, just a staging post on the journey that has become known as the northern arm of the Fairfield Horseshoe, so still feeling energetic I continued to Heron Pike, the next summit on the ridge, where I turned back. The clouds unfolded to offer me a fine vista over the great lakes to the south, with Morecambe Bay and the Coniston Fells in the distance.

Just after the summit, I turned downhill determined to visit Alcock Tarn. The clouds had completely gone and everything looked clear, every crack in the crags finely delineated. I sat for a long while on the shores of the tarn, letting the cares of the lowland world ease away. Lake District tarns are good for that, oases of peace in a troubled world. I lay back in the sunshine and read the words of William Palmer.

His Lakeland was still here on the high ground, even if much of the way of life he would have known had disappeared. The waters of the tarn lapped gently against its banks and the fiercer falling waters of Greenhead Gill echoed up from its narrow valley.

Does time really progress onwards? I often wonder. Is William Palmer still alive and caught in his time as I am now. Closing my eyes and listening to the eternal sounds of Lakeland, I felt as if I might reach out and shake Palmer by the hand. There is a real feeling that you might grasp the very concept of eternity when you are alone in the mountains.

I dwelt on that as I took the very steep zigzag path down to Greenhead Gill. The gradient of the valley and the multitude of waterfalls were very impressive, at their best after the heavy rain of previous days. The sound of running waters echoed through my mind as I walked back into Grasmere.

Borders

All his distinguished life the writer John Buchan noticed what he called sanctuaries - places in the wild where a man might hide from pursuers, finding these hidden places many times amidst the hills of Scotland. In his novel *Midwinter* he makes that strange Oxfordshire lowland Otmoor a sanctuary, the covert headquarters of the eponymous hero and his band of secret followers. In later years, when Governor-General of Canada, he took delight in spying out hidden valleys when flying over the vast wildernesses below.

But I suspect his first feeling of a sanctuary was in the high hills above Broughton, in the Scottish Borders. Buchan came to Broughton most summers as a child to stay at the farmhouse home of his grandparents. It was probably the most idyllic period of his life, the long summer hours spent walking in the hills, fly-fishing, helping around the farm, or just resting on the banks of the River Tweed.

In his adult years he often returned and the countryside of the Tweed provided the setting for much of his early writing. The white-coated farmhouse of his Masterton grandparents stands still on the main street of Broughton village, though it is now a private home. Not far away is the ruined kirk that he was to portray so vividly in his novel *Witchwood*. Here his younger sister, who died in childhood, and several of his relatives are buried. In the hills above I found a sanctuary that might have made quite an impression on his youthful mind.

The now quiet road running through Broughton was once the main road from Edinburgh to the border with England. Along this way marched the Jacobite army of Bonnie Prince Charlie. In Buchan's time the last of the drovers travelled its length, taking sheep and cattle to the sales fairs in the south. I thought of these past travellers as I left Broughton and followed the old road for a short distance before taking a steep and winding lane eastwards to Broughton Hall. This impressive castle-like building stands on the site of the home of John Murray, secretary to Prince Charlie during the Jacobite rebellion of 1745-6. This historical connection of Broughton must have appealed to the young Buchan, for Murray's wife features in one of his earliest novels *A Lost Lady of Old Years.*

Above the Hall is Shepherd's Cottage, a lonely homestead on the edge of much wilder countryside. Passing through a gate the softer green of the valley is left behind and the open ground of the hill lies ahead. It was October and the autumn colours were at their best on a dry and sunny day.

After crossing the Hollows Burn, I took a sharp route to the summit of Clover Law. The climb was steeper than I'd anticipated, the hills about me rounded and bulbous. But as always in hill walking it was surprising how quickly I made height. To the west and below were stretches of enclosed heathland and fields, the line of an ancient drove road and the distant town of Biggar. As I lay on the summit of Clover Law, a bee worked the last of the heather, crows cawed nearby and a kestrel hovered over the valley of Broughton Hope, where the Hollows Burn flows.

As I watched the hawk seeking out its prey, seemingly stuck in the air at my level, I became aware at just how hidden the valley below it was. A sharp turn at the southern end concealed this stretch of the landscape even from the Shepherd's Cottage. Before the days of aircraft it would have been hard to see, except from the neighbouring slopes. Buchan probably discovered this valley in early childhood and it may well have been the first of his many sanctuaries. As I looked down I could imagine the youthful author lying by the burn, perhaps even spinning the first of his yarns or contemplating the essays in his delightful early collection, the appropriately titled *Scholar Gipsies*.

I fancied how delightful it would be to pitch a camp at some time above the burn in the valley. Just the sight of it fevered my imagination. It was just the place where Covenanters might have hidden in those long religious disputes of the seventeenth century, or where border reivers would conceal stolen cattle. A few sheep grazed the heather on the hill slopes. It may well have been so in Buchan's time. It's interesting that even a lover of lonesome places like Buchan occasionally had feelings of dread if enclosed river valleys had no signs of animal life at all.

A sharp descent brought me to Corriemuir Hass, a tiny pass between Clover Law and the pleasantly named hill called Broomy Side. An old track went westwards at this point, but I turned to the east, following a path which is now part of the John Buchan Way, an excellent explorative trail running from Peebles to Broughton, highlighting areas of interest in the author's early life along its thirteen miles. But I wanted to continue my circuit of some of the Broughton Heights, so left the Way as an expedition for another day.

A steep climb brought me to the summit of Hammer Head, as dramatic in its steep sides and look as in its name. Having just come down from the Highlands, it felt strange to be amongst hills that had mostly anglicised names. Hammer Head was, like many of the Broughton Heights, round and smooth, though with some patches of grey scree. The climb up its northern edge was very steep, but the going was easy and I was soon sitting by the little summit cairn sipping tea.

All around were the border hills, like a wallowing sea turned to earth. The autumn colours were at their best with a myriad variety of brown and grey. As with all summits, I was saddened to leave and put off the moment until a band of low but dry cloud swept in from the west, hiding the sun and the highest of the distant summits.

A wonderful stretch of ridge walking brought me round to the lower top of Green Lairs and then to the higher point of Grey Yade. Just a few minutes after leaving Hammer Head, a great sweep of flat white cloud rolled in literally inches above my head. Below all was clear, but I could stretch up and watch all of the visibility around me disappear.

As I reached the wrecked stone wall on Trahenna Hill, the scene around me appeared wild and fantastic, like being on the very doorstep of some mythical heaven. It is hard to write down the inner feelings the climber feels at such a moment. It's as near to spiritual as it is possible to get - an existence away from the drudgeries of the world. The thrill of being so obviously between earth and sky reminded me just why I love hill walking so much. At such moments I can understand best what Richard Jefferies in *The Story of my Heart* meant when he lay down on a Wiltshire hilltop and recognised that 'eternity is now'.

After a few moments sitting on the old wall trying to capture in my notebook the feeling of the mist, my eye was taken with a movement on the wall. A strange-looking long legged spider crawled along one of the horizontal stones and on to the flap of my rucksack. Within a moment he was joined by a fellow spider which emerged out of a crack in the wall and then another, and another, until dozens of the tiny creatures began to emerge from other hidden recesses. I had never seen such a type of spider before. I moved and took my rucksack away, fearing that I might accidentally crush these denizens of the heights.

As I watched them the mist lifted and soon the clouds were scudding higher into the atmosphere, opening up the wide vista of the Broughton Heights. I followed the ridge path down over Cat Cleuch Head, losing height rapidly, with very good views over the imposing Broughton Place as I headed back to Broughton village. Descending to Shepherd's cottage, the sanctuary of Broughton Hope tucked itself away behind its concealing ring of hills.

~

Not long afterwards I decided to walk part of one of the old drove roads, so vividly described by John Buchan in his essay on the subject in *Scholar Gipsies*. Moreover, I chose a stretch of an old drover's route that Buchan would certainly have known, which runs from behind the old ruined kirk at Broughton to the village of Skirling.

It was a blazing hot May morning, every neighbouring border hill standing out with exceptional clarity, the air full of birdsong; skylarks danced above while from the valley brooks came the plaintive cries of peewit and curlew.

The drove road from Broughton is a stretch of unenclosed grass between meadows and wilder ground. That it exists at all, and has not been grabbed into the surrounding fields is a tribute to the memory and power of such an ancient way. As Buchan wrote, *This is the Drove Road, the way once used more than all the others when market-roads were rough and ill-kept and barred with toll-gates.*

It is a kind of miracle that such routes have survived, saying a lot for how the Borders have remained unspoiled. The conveyance of stock along these roads was once the major industry for borderers, both Scots and English. Buchan was fortunate to have lived at a time when some of the drove roads were still in use and he writes of his boyhood longing to be off with the drovers who passed the home of his grandparents. Any wayfarer could devote a whole walking career to following the many tracks that remain.

The distance between Broughton and Skirling is but a few miles and so I enjoyed the laziness of a short walk. These occasional strolls are one of the delights of vagabonding; being able to lie back in heather for hours at a time, just gazing at the sky, or watching the sheep graze and the kestrel hover. Very different from the drovers of old who had to combine the talents of driving the beasts swiftly to market, but without losing their bodyweight or wearing the animals down and making them unsaleable. They were a colourful crew as Buchan tells us:

These were a daring, godless race, deep drinkers all, fond of brawls and quick as fire to take offence. They were hardy too, sleeping out-of-doors and enduring the sternest rigours of our uncertain northern weather.

Buchan had a great admiration for such individuals, for though he was a son of the manse he had a daring and lawless side to his outwardly Presbyterian nature. His early stories and sketches are mostly about the working men of Tweeddale, the poachers, shepherds and gamekeepers; so different in tone from the clubland characters of his later novels. He draws them well in these first sketches, for he saw such people all around him in these Border hills. Now they are lost, just ghostly echoes to be imagined as you doze, as I did, against the banks and stone walls that line the drove road.

The route climbed uphill and then contoured a hill slope before reaching a stand of firs. For a moment I lost the obvious line of the path and I wandered down a sheep pasture in search of it, the animals moving away from me with protesting bleats. I leapt the Kirklawhill Burn, imagining the herds watering their stock along its banks, passed through a gate, and then climbed towards a stand of pines.

Looking back now, across to the sheep pasture, I could see a raised strip of harder ground that was obviously the route of the old drove road, though I suspect in dry seasons the herds would have spread out across the hillside, grazing as they were driven forth. The pines around me must have been planted since the heyday of the route, though the planter had shown a reverence for the route, lining the track and leaving a good clear way in between. Soon afterwards the road became very clearly defined as it passed a long house called Whinnybrae and headed down to the village of Skirling.

And an odd place it was, something like a southern English village transported into the Scottish scene, complete with a tree-shaded village green lined with cottages; at one side an "Arts and Crafts" house built in 1908 for Lord Carmichael. I sat on a bench for a long while, admiring this very rural scene, for this quiet corner of Scotland abounded with blossom and bluebells, and dozens of tits flew in and out of the trees above.

In the days of the drove road it was probably much busier, for the green would have been an ideal place to quarter the beasts for the night. I tried to see it through Buchan's eyes, imagining the drovers drinking, gambling and fighting in the surrounding cottages.

I returned the way I had come, thinking myself a drover heading towards the border with England. I was soon distracted by the sight of a drainage ditch absolutely crammed with tadpoles. I tried the old trick of letting the shadow of my walking stick fall across the water, causing the tadpoles to freeze, no doubt in case the shadow is that of a predator. It works every time and must be an instinct instilled in every tadpole that ever was.

The drove road seemed much clearer, heading in this direction, often with a drystone wall on one side and the lovely yellow of the broom on the other. I felt reluctant to complete the journey and slowed and halted more than usual, looking up often to the towers of Broughton Place and the Heights beyond, bringing back memories of my circuit of those beautiful tops.

In the Kirkyard at Broughton I sought out the grave of Buchan's sister Violet, who died in childhood. It was not her grave that made me feel sad, but one nearby which read "W. Taylor, Highland Light Infantry, killed 10th November 1918". As I looked around at the peaceful scene I could not help reflecting on the death of this poor boy, who died on the last full day of the Great War, and who, perhaps, had once roamed along the old drove road from Broughton to Skirling.

Navvies

Deep in the Scottish Highlands in the upper valley of the River Leven is truly wild country, caught between the great rift of Glencoe and the mountains of Lochaber. But this is also an industrial landscape. The village of Kinlochleven came about as a centre for the manufacture of aluminium, powered by the stored waters of the Leven held behind the long wall of the Blackwater Dam.

The inspiration for my hill walk out to the great dam occurred several years before, some miles beyond Fort William at Glenfinnan. On a very wet day I'd called in at the National Trust for Scotland's visitor centre in search of something to read. A lady assistant recommended the recently republished novels of navvy life *Children of the Dead End* and its sequel *Moleskin Joe*, by the much neglected author Patrick MacGill. As the rain poured down that evening I sat by the fireside in the tiny cottage in Benderloch and avidly read these tales of navvying in early twentieth century Scotland.

Although presented as novels the books are largely autobiographical, telling how the young MacGill worked on farmsteads and industrial sites around Ireland and Scotland before journeying on foot the hundred miles between Greenock and the dam construction works on the Leven. That trek itself was quite arduous with the two navvies having to steal a boat to cross the Clyde, before they could even begin their long walk through the Highlands.

They had roamed on through inhospitable countryside, having to steal or scrounge for food, MacGill literally barefooted as they took the last steps of their journey over the rugged terrain where the workers lived:

A sleepy hollow lay below; and within it a muddle of shacks, roofed with tarred canvas, and built of driven piles, were huddled together in bewildering confusion. These were surrounded by puddles, heaps of disused woods, tins, bottles, and all manner of discarded rubbish. Some of the shacks had windows, most of them had none; some had doors facing north, some south; everything was in a most haphazard condition, and it looked as if the buildings had dropped out of the sky by accident, and were just allowed to remain where they had fallen.

It was here that MacGill was to live and work for months on end, at the great dam itself and on the route of the pipelines down to Kinlochleven. The Blackwater navvies blew up and carved out great chunks of mountainside in one of the most exposed areas of the Highlands by night and day, in midge-ridden hot weather and during weeks of blizzards and lashing rain. Men were crammed dozens to a hut, often drunk or fighting over the consequences of a gambling match. Then with the completion of the dam they were paid off and marched away to the next job leaving the remnants of where they had lived behind.

Well, not all of them marched away. Accidents during their labours were common and a number of the navvies died, to be buried below the dam in a lonely and most atmospheric graveyard.

The aluminium works at Kinlochleven are closed now, though the workers' houses remain in the deep vale between those high mountains. The waters of the great Blackwater Dam provide power for hydro-electricity. Some of the buildings of the old works have been given over to leisure interests, outdoor centres with climbing walls. But it feels as if the ghosts of those navvies remain in the long valley down from the dam.

Clouds thundered up the glen as I set out from Kinlochleven, though it remained dry and intermittently sunny for my first mile. The initial stage of my route was part of the

West Highland Way, that very popular long distance walk from Glasgow to Fort William. I tramped the winding and steep track through thick birchwoods up the side of the glen, at first beside the huge pipeline from the dam that curved down the hillside.

As I reached higher ground the clouds delivered short but heavy and cold showers, though the sun in between the downpours warmed me and made it unnecessary to wear my much hated waterproof clothing. The clouds were high above the mountain summits and there were fine views across to the Mamores, that great range of mountains that huddle up to the highest of all British summits - Ben Nevis.

The dam proved to be further away than I'd imagined. I lost height into a deep valley, which had to be regained on its eastern side. It was close to a lonely cottage on the valley's topmost edge that I found the conduit again, now covered by an earthen flat track above the pipes, making easier progress as it contoured the walls of the glen.

You cannot help but be amazed at this astonishing feat of engineering, on a par with the construction of the dam itself. The Blackwater navvies worked the pipeline's route out of solid rock, much of it precipitous cliff. Where waterfalls tumbled down the slopes of the glen, narrow bridges carried the pipeline high over the rushing waters. Their slippery track took me sometimes deep into the hillside, then as suddenly out above incredible drops.

Far below the white waters of Leven crashed down the glen, supplemented by what seemed to be hundreds of waterfalls from the surrounding hills. Apart from the silver of the birches, the whole landscape appeared brown and golden - those rich colours of a highland October. A stag bellowed from the woodland lining the banks of the river, his unearthly cry echoing miles into the mountains. The sound must have been very familiar to the navvies as they slaved away, day and night on their perilous perches between the river and the sky.

It took three hours of walking before the dam came into view. I think I had expected something narrower and taller, rather than the long grey line of wall that traversed the head of the glen. I had a feeling of profound unease as I stood in its shadow, and not I think just because of the millions of tons of water held above me. Peculiar thudding noises, crashes and booms seemed to come from the heart of its great wall, for all the world as though the navvies were still at work deep inside its stones.

Some of the navvies never left their workplace. They lie in a tiny but atmospheric burial ground below the dam, a great mound of earth that they themselves probably shifted into place. Simple headstones in ragged lines mark the last resting place of a couple of dozen of Patrick MacGill's contemporaries. I walked between them reading the names which were mostly Scottish and Irish. Some bore nicknames such as "Darkie Cunningham", others had no name at all, perhaps bits of body unrecognisable in death after a rock fall or an accident with explosives.

There was a grave of a woman, and a more recent headstone from 1978 with the epitaph "These Are My Mountains". I wondered if this perhaps was a navvy who had died a more peaceful death seventy years on from his fellows but who sought to lie with them in this loneliest of graveyards, or just someone who had a fellow feeling with these half-forgotten individuals.

MacGill relates how some workers perished in blizzards as they made a desperate journey across the mountains in search of liquor at the Kingshouse Inn on the skirts of Rannoch Moor, their bones lying in the heather to this day. We talk now of hard work and a tough existence, but what do we know of either compared to the existence of the navvies who laboured day and night on freezing mountainsides, lashed with rain and snow and attacked by swarms of midges on warmer summer days?

They lived hard, worked to extremes, fought the landscape and each other, and occasionally died in this out of the way place. Nothing remains of the shanty town, described so vividly by Patrick MacGill, but the refuse pits where broken shovels and rusty food tins remind us of the courageous and colourful individuals who made this desolate place their temporary home.

I felt humbled as I stood among the headstones for I know I will never have to toil as hard as the navvies who lay by my feet. The mountains for me are a challenge and a pleasure, not rock to be confronted and worked away. As I stood there the great belt of cloud that had hung for so long over Loch Leven began to head inland towards me, bringing the promise of rain. I bowed my head in silent tribute to these brave individuals and then walked away without looking back.

A track took me to the conduit and I headed back to Kinlochleven. And it was just then that I had one of those weird experiences that seem natural when you are high in the lonely mountains, but appear to be irrational, unexplainable, when back at home.

As I approached a turn in the pipeline track I heard some men in conversation ahead of me. They were talking loudly, their voices echoing back from the side of the mountain. I turned the corner but there was no one in sight and the talking had stopped.

But a few hundred yards on it began again, seemingly right in front of me, then in the air all around. There was a strong masculine voice speaking with an Irish accent. I could barely make out the words, but I knew the conversation was not in

English. More likely Erse or perhaps Scottish Gaelic. There was one very loud speaker and two fainter answering voices.

I saw nothing, but it felt as though the loudest of the men was standing right next to me and his fellows some little distance down the slope. The air seemed to tingle as the voices grew louder, and then melted away. Suddenly, as I descended, the voices stopped as though the spell was broken. The strange atmosphere was gone.

I am aware that sounds travel in peculiar ways in the mountains, and it's certainly not the first time I have heard conversations in this way. But I know that these sounds were not *inside* my head, but external. And they were too close to me and vivid to be the carried conversations of distant hillwalkers.

Were the voices some ghostly echo of the Blackwater navvies? It's true that I had been in a very atmospheric place that had moved me, and the navvies were heavy in my thoughts. But I remain convinced that the sounds were not some imaginative projection. I do think that it is possible for great emotions to be imprinted on landscapes and played back in the same way that we listen and watch recorded music and pictures on disc. There is something that we do not yet understand about these matters, but they are inexplicable only in the sense that our science has not yet found a way to bring them to our understanding.

The showers became more frequent as the band of cloud rolled overhead, turning into a fierce downpour as I breasted the last valley before Kinlochleven. In the birchwoods I passed three hikers huddled away from the rain in a stretch of furze, looking thoroughly dispirited. I waved a hand but they just looked miserable in return. As I walked into Kinlochleven some lads approached and asked if I had encountered three of their friends overdue whilst walking the stretch of the West Highland Way from Rannoch Moor. I pointed them in the right direction and then sat in the pouring rain on the banks of the Leven thinking about Patrick MacGill's description of the day the navvies of the Blackwater dam were paid off and they marched away:

A great silence fell on the party. The nailed shoes rasping on the hard earth, and the half-whispered curse of some falling man as he tripped over a hidden boulder, were the only sounds that could be heard in the darkness. And down the face of the mountain the ragged army tramped slowly on.

Stravaiging

Some of the best experiences in the outdoors are on those walks which are unplanned in detail, and where you find yourself in new places quite inadvertently.

Sometimes, a relatively modest walk becomes a longer expedition, taking you to places you never dreamt existed. You find new trackways, see the lonely places where folk dwell, and discover matchless views that you cannot have imagined.

On a bright morning, I was dropped by motoring relatives in Gleann Salach, near Benderloch in Argyllshire, with the intention of climbing Beinn Bhreac - the speckled mountain - a relatively modest height, but with promised views over much of that wild area.

I climbed over a sheep fence and made my way up the hillside, a mixture of heather bog and rock, not particularly steep but it felt a long way to the top. Like many Scottish mountains there seemed to be several false summits and I had that feeling of never getting to the true top. I expected midges, but in fact the botheration was swarms of hungry flies. I pulled my hat down over my head and rolled down my sleeves in a pointless attempt to ward off their persistent attacks. I had encountered these flies before in mountain districts, but none so determined to bite. I tried every which way to outmanoeuvre them. I swung a map case through their hungry ranks; dived to the ground with my rucksack over my head; ran furiously up and down the slope. Then I just resigned myself to their company and plodded on to the top.

Funnily enough, they cleared away as I reached the summit cairn. I felt as though I'd passed some sort of initiative test, and that my persistence had appeased these villainous guardians of the mountain, who now let me be. Beinn Bhreac is seldom climbed by mountaineers in Scotland, or so I'm told, but I can't think why. Its views are as good as from many of the loftier summits around.

As I looked down there was a broad stretch of beautiful Loch Etive, from the Connel Bridge to Taynuilt, then the mighty peaks of Ben Cruachan, my very first Munro of the year before. As I looked I remembered that wondrous day when I summited in dense cloud. Into view came the dark lochs inland from Oban, then the islands of Mull and Eriska; before me the distant mountains of Morven and Appin, all strung around a great necklace of silver water; sea and sea lochs seeming to hold this landscape together, mirroring so many mountainous reflections. Along the range was the greater height of Beinn Sgulaird, which I intended to climb a few days hence, and for which my ascent of Beinn Bhreac was a kind of reconnoitre. Then in the far distance, the hills of Glencoe and Ben Nevis, towering over all.

The summit cairn of Beinn Bhreac is several feet high, and the top of the mountain broken and rocky. Skylarks hovered and whirled above my head, and the sound of a cuckoo echoed up from the glen. Just down from the top a stretch of heather stank of fox and my presence sent a red deer hind careering downhill.

I wondered what to do next, having attained the top in less time than I'd envisaged. I had to be back at the cottage in Benderloch for a late tea. But, as I sat on the summit of Beinn Bhreac, the thought of going straight down again seemed to be too modest an expedition. The skies were clear and the sheer joy of being in the Highlands suggested that I find a circuitous route back home. As I looked at the map there seemed to be intriguing forest rides through Barcaldine Forest and I considered that I might journey along them back to the village.

The conifer plantations swept across the lower slopes of the mountain. I'm not a fan of conifers on such a massive scale and avoid them as much as possible. Apart from along the forest rides, negotiation of conifered mountain sides is usually far more trouble than it is worth. I forgot that thought as I headed swiftly downhill through heather and bracken.

I was reminded of it within the hour.

The first problem was the massively high deer fence that formed the boundary between the forest and the open mountain. It resembled, albeit without any barbed wire along the top, those fences that you see in prisoner of war films. The conifers lay hard against the far side, making a crossing impossible at that point. I wandered a couple of hundred yards in each direction, in the vain hope that there was a gate.

Well, I couldn't find one.

After following the fence for about a third of a mile, I did however discover a stretch of fence that was clear on the far side. So I climbed, one foot on the wire and the other leg shinning up a fencing post. It was easier going up than coming down on the far side, where the cut branches of trees stuck up like spears, catching my clothing and rucksack straps, making the descent a difficult and painful experience.

But there was what looked like a clear ride heading downhill and this I took, only to find it came to a dead end after a hundred yards. The trees here were of middle years and the lowest branches were just a couple of feet off the ground, each tree entangled with all of its immediate neighbours. The thought of having to climb the deer fence again drove me onwards, pushing my way between the trees, occasionally crawling in the dark underworld on the thick layer of fallen pine needles. The heady scent of the trees on such a hot day was overwhelming and I felt caged and stifled in a strange dark world.

I should have known better. Short cuts rarely work in the outdoor world, almost never in conifer woods. Yet I will try them, as I have tried to force my way through conifer forests from Dartmoor to the Grampians. Like multiple marriages, crashing through conifers in search of a route is a triumph of hope over experience. Eventually, I leaned against a particularly stubborn branch which swayed, gave way, and sent me rolling down the gravelled bank of a contouring forest ride.

I lay at the bottom for several minutes, red with heat, scratches and embarrassment, too tired even to pull the flask of water out of my rucksack. But my struggle was to lead to a serendipitous reward. A noise came from the conifer line, a rustling amid the undergrowth. Then, with a slide of gravel, a tiny creature shot into the middle of the ride and gazed around. It was a pine marten. I'd obviously disturbed its diurnal rest with my noisy descent. It had waited until it thought I had passed before seeking quieter shelter. Fortunately, I was downwind of the animal and huddled into a fold of the bank. The marten looked all around, but didn't seem to see me. He sniffed the air, then walked very slowly across the ride and into the conifers on the far side. I sat there for a while, counting my good fortune in seeing this elusive creature. It made the tiresome struggle through the trees worthwhile.

I walked on along the ride in the general direction of Barcaldine, then I had to zigzag back on myself along another forest ride for a half mile before I reached the slopes of Gleann Dubh - the Black Glen - and dark it was beneath the conifers that now covered most of the valley. There is something about walking on forest rides that makes you feel really thirsty. Whether it is the lack of a breeze or the sun beating down on the hardened surface I'm not sure. But in Barcaldine I poured back drink with great abandon, leaving only enough to ensure the quenching of thirst on the remainder of my journey.

In theory this was easy, a tramp along the main road towards Benderloch and Oban. But as the traffic sped by I was inclined to avoid as much as possible the busy public highway. Looking at the map, I noticed a track from Achanreir to very near Benderloch, and this I decided to follow.

It was more promising than I'd imagined. A signpost near the junction with the lane told me that it was an ancient corpse road, along which the dead would have made one final journey. These are not uncommon. The road through Gleann Salach, where I had begun my journey, was a famous corpse route. Colin Campbell of Glenure, whose assassination forms the historical basis of Robert Louis Stevenson's novel *Kidnapped*, had been taken along it for burial in the priory at Ardchattan, on the shores of Loch Etive. I've followed many such ways of the dead elsewhere in Scotland, as well as on Dartmoor, Lakeland, and in the Yorkshire Dales. They usually have an undoubted atmosphere, particularly when they wind through remote countryside.

I followed its length for some time without meeting anyone, though at one point the barking of dogs, alerted to the sound of my steps, echoed over the hillside. There was a dogs' home somewhere in the trees. Apart from that disturbance it was pleasant going. At last I came to a section of the track that was blocked by woodmen clearing trees. They waved a friendly greeting and halted operations as I walked past. Whether I followed the track to its conclusion, I'm still not sure, for after a pleasing mile or two I found myself out on the road again.

Cars whizzed by and I was glad to turn into a quieter lane, soon coming within view of the Black Castle of Barcaldine. This tower is not in fact black, though it looks it in the shade. Its reputation as an outpost of Clan Campbell power was black enough. It was here that the Chief of the Clan MacDonald of Glencoe was deliberately delayed on his way to Inverary, making him late in swearing fealty to King William of Orange, and occasioning the bloody massacre of Glencoe.

The tower has been renovated by modern-day members of the Campbell family and now offers a friendlier welcome as a venue for weddings and a halt for the bed and breakfast trade.

For me, weary and hot from my travels, it marked the beginning of the end of my journey. A mile along the lane brought me to the familiar old white cottage, where I might sit in a shady room and read books about Highland history. I always sleep well after such journeys, tired from the exertions of the day and free of worry. It is then that I know best that the open road, the lonely woodlands, and the open mountainsides are where I'm meant to be.

~

The old Jacobite song begins with the words "Cam ye by Atholl, lad with the philabeg, down by the Tummel and banks of the Garry". I never hear it without being mentally transported to the beautiful wild country north of Pitlochry; the great wooded pass of Killiecrankie, the mountainous slopes of Ben Vrackie, and the deer-haunted braes of Atholl. Places of a thousand memories, where I long to be again and again.

Pitlochry is a town of great charm and friendliness, a place to linger and a centre for some beautiful walks. Ben Vrackie is *its* mountain, in the same way that Zermatt claims the Matterhorn, or Fort William Ben Nevis. Not that you can see the Ben from the middle of town, you need to journey to the heights beyond or across the river to achieve a good view, but it is Pitlochry's mountain none the less, the backdrop to the town as you approach from the south.

Ben Vrackie has the reputation of being an easy mountain, one whose top may be achieved even by tourists. But that is to do that lovely mountain a great disservice, for it is a good hard climb from the town, and its summit offers one of the finest viewpoints in Perthshire. The circuit over the mountain and then back to town by way of the Pass of Killiecrankie has long been a favourite of mine, since I first journeyed that way so many years ago.

A good track leads from Moulin village and out on to the open hillside to Ben Vrackie, and what a track it is for views as it climbs gradually towards the Ben, great sweeping vistas over the town and the great wide valley of the River Tummel. Ben Vrackie takes its name from the Gaelic for "speckled", and I once assumed that it took this from the folds of rock across its summit. But as the paths around catch the sun the ground beneath your feet glistens with microscopic dusts of quartz and I've come to the conclusion that this is what is meant. Whatever, the paths offer an easy approach to the foot of the summit cliffs above a little dammed lochan called Loch a Choire.

I first walked this way one June, on a fine hot day, with skylarks almost invisible to sight, but whose song echoed across the grouse moors below the mountain. I saw few grouse that day, though the ones I did disturb skimmed the heather with annoyed cries as I disturbed their rest. The steeply climbing track that the tourists take edges round to the east of the sharp cliffs above the lochan, but I took a route to the top that involved a bit more scrambling. This offered some thrilling climbing on good rock and steep heather banks, gaining height quickly and making the dark waters of the lochan seem a long way below. It took me a half hour to get to the summit, always a heavenly moment as you feel that something almost mystical has been achieved.

I lay down in the shelter of the viewpoint indicator on the top, and looked abroad at the great panorama that lay all around; the woods and pastures of Strath Tay and Tummel, the great wooded gash of Killiecrankie, the summits of the Grampians, to north and west, some still snow-capped, as they reached over towards Rannoch Moor and Glencoe. It was a sight to take the breath away.

I thought about that distant day in June on a later climb to the summit of Ben Vrackie, a hard journey against a freezing gale from Killiecrankie. Approaching the mountain from the north it was all I could do to stand up. I fought my way across bogs and deep patches of heather, before climbing the steep slopes of the lower summit of Meall an Daimh. At one point was a broad band of lying snow, unmarked by footsteps, trapped in the shelter of a shallow corrie. It felt almost intrusive to walk across the virgin snow, but delightful to do so, for it was crisp and hardly gave at all under my weight.

How wonderful to be on the mountains in the snow. There is something pure and elemental in mountain tramps in such conditions. It is a world away from the boredom and thanklessness of the workaday world. Never have I felt so alive as in the mountains in wild weather.

There was no one on the mountain on that wintry day, except me. As I rested on the top of the snow band, the clouds parted and threw open a view of one distant snow covered peak after another. A raven croaked amid the boulders above me, and suddenly a stag and a herd of red deer hinds broke cover from the shoulder of the mountain, streaming downhill like the waters of a tawny river. I watched them with a sense of wonder, that there could be such moments in a lifetime, such a reckoning with the wilderness. I climbed to the top of Meall an Daimh and lay back in the snow and heather, thinking of that first June expedition and the many times I'd climbed these hills since.

One autumn day I'd stood for a while on the rocky edge of Meall an Daimh and looked across to the higher summit of Ben Vrackie, then climbed down into the lower ground between the two. As I turned and looked back to where I had stood a few minutes earlier, I saw myself still there, as clear and as solid as I am in life.

I watched for several minutes, thinking at first that it must be some other walker with identical clothes and rucksack, and with a passing resemblance to me.

But I knew it could not be so, for no one could have attained the top that quickly without me seeing their approach. The figure was in exactly the same place that I had been just a while before, looking in the same direction towards the summit of the Ben. I remained transfixed, watching what seemed to be my own ghost for some minutes, then as suddenly as this vision had appeared, it was gone. I cannot explain that peculiar apparition. I am sure that it was not an hallucination, some projection from my own mind, but a being as temporarily solid as the rocks around.

Such things happen in the wild places, and not just to the credulous. There is something elemental, some phenomenon that is wholly natural, but which the human race doesn't yet understand. Perhaps we encounter it most in the mountains because we let our emotional guard down and accept nature and its creations in the raw.

On that first time to the summit of Ben Vrackie I sat and had my lunch, my back to the rocks, admiring the view over Pitlochry. I'd scarcely begun before the mountain goats arrived, two of them; both obviously used to the lunchtime habits of mountain stravaigers. They would have eaten my rucksack if I'd let them. The goats have gone now but they were legendary in their time, much beloved by the many hillwalkers who topped Ben Vrackie. They had much of my lunch and I've missed seeing them on my many returns to the mountain.

On the descent down towards Killiecrankie there are fine views across to the old Jacobite battlefield, though it's somewhat marred by the new A9 trunk road. It was on the slopes above the River Garry that the Jacobite army under "Bonnie" Dundee, or Claverhouse, or "Bloody Clavers", depending on your political perspective, drew up to await the government army commanded by Lord Mackay, which had to negotiate the narrow path through the Pass of Killiecrankie, on what turned out to be a very bloody day in 1689.

Dundee had the benefit of holding the high ground, which facilitated a highland charge downhill on to the poorly positioned government army. Mackay's army was thoroughly routed, fleeing in terror back down the pass, one soldier jumping the Garry in one massive leap as he was pursued by angry highlanders. The Jacobite cause took little comfort from this victory, for Dundee was mortally wounded at the very moment of his triumph and the rising faded away.

I'm fascinated by battlefields and have explored a great many. Given the history of the British race there can scarcely be many corners of our landscape that were not soaked in blood.

The battlefields we know about must be the tip of an iceberg, for the locations of perhaps hundreds of early battles or minor skirmishes have been lost to us.

I think there is an atmosphere on a battlefield, that *something* in their locality is changed for ever by those hours of slaughter. I once talked to someone on Dartmoor who, walking through a wooded valley, heard the sounds of some ancient conflict going on all around them, though he saw nothing. I remember being told, before my first visit to Culloden that the birds do not sing over the battlefield. It isn't true, for I've heard them sing there most delightfully, and I've always found it a light and airy place on shiny days. But I was once there on a dark and gloomy morning and thought it most oppressive. I think it all depends on your own mood at the time.

I seem to recall that on that first walk I wandered up to Blair Atholl, so that I might see another kind of battleground, from the days of the access wars, the place being Glen Tilt, the long glen that climbs between the Grampian Mountains from the white-painted Blair Castle, the ancestral home of the dukes of Atholl. It was in Glen Tilt, a particularly scenic part of the duke's 200,000 acres, that one of the most memorable of Victorian access battles took place. The track through Glen Tilt, the only direct route from Blair to Braemar and Deeside, had been a drovers' route for centuries and was much used by the growing number of recreational walkers, until the sixth duke began to forbid public access. I've written an account of the subsequent conflict with the hillwalkers and stravaigers of Scotland in my book *The Compleat Trespasser*. It's quite a yarn, as fascinating in its way as the Jacobite battle two centuries before.

The track back to Pitlochry through the heavily wooded Pass of Killiecrankie is as narrow as it was on the day that

Mackay's army marched along it, high above the roaring whisky-coloured waters of the River Garry.

The Pass has always been one of the gateways to the Highlands, hence the building of Blair Castle. In the 1700s General Wade constructed the first proper road through Killiecrankie, fragments of which may still be seen in the car park of the National Trust for Scotland visitor centre. The railway from the South to Inverness takes a dramatic route this way, as does the modern A9. But the best way to experience the Pass is by journeying on foot along the original track.

I first walked it in the spring, when the leaves on the trees had their first green freshness, the river banks covered with such a profusion of wild flowers that my journey was a long series of admiring pauses. Red squirrels chattered in the boughs above, and the songs of the birds competed with the crashing roar of the river. So narrow is the path that it's hard to imagine an army marching this way, there is room only for a couple of men abreast. I thought it strange that Dundee bothered to wait for his foes to march through and form ranks on the open ground beyond, when he could so easily have ambushed his enemies in the Pass. He was, perhaps, too sporting for his own good.

I've walked the Pass of Killiecrankie many times, but never lost my sense of wonder at the spectacular passage of the Garry. I can see myself now, on that first walk, tired after my long journey, but thrilled at the ascent of Ben Vrackie, the walk up to Blair Atholl, and this magnificent finale through the Pass.

Above Pitlochry is Loch Faskally, a reservoir which gathers the waters of the Garry and the Tummel. I find most reservoirs unattractive, with their artificial shorelines scarring what was once pretty countryside, but I *do* like Loch Faskally; somehow it works as a complement to the wild scene around.

A path from Killiecrankie winds around its banks and takes the walker back into Pitlochry, but I always remember my first time there, when I was staying in the hillside village of Moulin, crossing the railway line and walking up the brae to the Cuilc, the pond filled with hungry ducks and waterfowl, where I sat for a while on a bench and wished that I never had to leave such beautiful countryside. In moments of tiredness I sometimes close my eyes and picture elements of that walk so vividly that I can feel the mountain air on my face, hear the rush of the river, and sense the tranquillity of the woodlands in that peaceful glen.

Resting

Some of the best memories of these walks have been at the resting spots, the places where I might halt for refreshment or just to admire the view and to rest. All such stops are memorable in different ways and hundreds come to mind as I think back.

They don't necessarily have to be spectacular, offering wide views across miles of countryside. They can be exactly the opposite; the banks of a hollow way where I huddled down under the trees to drink tea with the pouring rain dripping on to my waterproofs, or the bench on a village green where I paused to watch the world go by, the promenade of a seaside resort or the hidden alleyways of town and city.

The mountain summits speak for themselves in my memories as places to linger. Walking is obviously not an end in itself. You walk in order to get to places, joyful though the journey might be. But the halts along the way are an essential part of the experience. Not just as places to consume food and drink but as rests, spaces where body and mind may be refreshed. The break from the walk, for me, is often an opportunity to think, or sometimes not to think - just to be.

If solitary roaming is a kind of moving meditation, then these pauses are moments for reflection, time off from the hurried and harrying world that is life in this twenty-first century.

To lie on your back and gaze at the sky can bring true peace, free of intruding conversations and the ill-thought out actions of others. Such moments are not a luxury in life but a positive necessity. On a clear day, resting on the great slope of a mountain or the green turf of downland you can almost feel the rotation of the earth, as though time itself doesn't exist and there really is just you and the universe. In his mystical book *The Story of My Heart*, Richard Jefferies discovers the depths of such moments:

There were grass-grown tumuli on the hills to which of old I used to walk, sit down at the foot of one of them, and think. Some warrior had been interred there in the ante-historic times. The sun of the summer morning shone on the dome of sward, and the air came softly up from the wheat below, the tips of the grasses swayed as it passed sighing faintly, it ceased, and the bees hummed by to the thyme and heathbells. I became absorbed in the glory of the day, the sunshine, the sweet air, the yellowing corn turning from its sappy green to summer's noon of gold, the lark's song like a waterfall in the sky.

Jefferies identifies with the man buried in the tumulus, someone who would have known the scene two millennia before, and he realises that time and eternity are imposed concepts that have little to do with the feelings that people get when they let themselves absorb the reality of the earth.

"Eternity is now!" Jefferies remarks. There is, he suggests, no separation from the past. The truth of the world is continuous and all around.

I've felt similar feelings when alone and in the hills. The dramas of the world, its conflicts and wars, its terrors and unhappiness have faded away - at least in my mind - in the times I've rested, pleasantly tired from a walk, in the lonely places. And the thought has often occurred to me that if everyone in the world could find such ease, then the conflicts, the wars, and the lack of happiness might be expelled from the human psyche for ever.

The greatest moments of peace of mind I've ever known have been in these interludes during my many walks. Some of the resting spots are heart places to me; locations I can journey to in my mind during the frustrating times of modern living, and see and feel and hear and absorb the sounds of the quieter world around.

These heart places are diverse kinds of landscape. There is a bench at the top of Arundel Park arrived at by a walk up a gentle slope, where I've often rested and soaked up the peace of the downlands and the wide views over the valley of the Arun and the flooded bowl of Amberley Wild Brooks. There is a tiny waterfall near Ballachulish, where on a sunny day in May I lay back on a boulder, my feet being soaked by water which just a little while before had been snow on the slopes of Beinn a' Fheiter. There is an old tree in the woodlands of Hole Common, near Lyme Regis, where I've halted for lunch on numerous occasions, watching the deer if I've been early enough in the day. Near to the Black Lochs of Kilvaree in Argyll is a ruined dwelling, below a precariously perched boulder, where I have paused in sunshine and in storm. And there is the quiet resting spot on the shores of Loch Lochy where I drummed up refreshing tea on a still autumn evening.

These are just a very few of the heart places that have lived in my mind since I first discovered them. Places I will return to again and again, whether on physical expeditions, or just as journeys in my thoughts and dreams. These are the unexpected riches of a wayfaring life.

Summit Fever

Climbing towards the clouds on Ben Cruachan. A fine day as the Pass of Brander and Loch Awe are left behind. Then up to the col between the twin summits and then a very rocky path to the top. And all the while are fine views over much of the Scottish Highlands. Then out towards the Hebrides to the high ground of Mull. A feeling of mightiness all around, for Cruachan is a mighty peak.

And then, just a dozen yards from the top I entered the base of a cloud and entered a white world where nothing existed more than a couple of yards away. On the top of Cruachan I sat down weary from the long haul. I might as well have been in some parallel universe of whiteness, the only sign of life being me. A feeble explorer into a world greater than myself.

Sitting on the little area that is the summit, I could have been the only living creature left in the world. I crawled towards the northern edge where cliffs plunge down towards Coire Chat, the Allt Garbh and Glen Noe. I thought, even then, what a fine setting it would make for a thriller. Years later, I put an assassin with a rifle in this very landscape in my novel *Balmoral Kill*. Being alone on a summit, particularly when the rest of existence is blotted out, feeds the imagination.

And there was another feeling as well, something I've noticed time and again when I've reached the top of a hill after a long climb. I call it Summit Fever. It's hard to put the sensation into words, but it's a kind of high. However tired I might be from the climb I feel a sudden rush of energy, a tirelessness. A feeling that goes beyond human strength and power.

But there's more to summit fever than that. It's difficult to put into words, but there's an emotional soar as well as a physical surge. As though you aren't quite the same human being you were at the foot of the ascent.

I've noticed, time and again, a reluctance to leave the summit once you are there. On a clear day there may be wide views, but even if there aren't, even if the top is fog-bound or storm-battered, it becomes very hard to tear yourself away. It's never so bad if you're heading along a ridge to a higher summit, your soul knows you're aiming for the attainment of some higher place.

But if you are to go back down, well, not only is there a feeling of loss, but the physical tiredness can come back very quickly. It's no surprise to me that so many mountain accidents happen on the descent.

So what is it about summits?

A mystic might say that the top of a mountain is a 'thin place' – where parallel worlds meet. Where you might be at the same time in two existences at once. It's interesting that quantum physicists are now suggesting similar possibilities. I wouldn't rule anything out. The one thing I've learned in all these years being out in the natural world is that the whole of existence is a sheer bloody miracle and that we are not a small percentage towards even a slight understanding of the universe.

In his inspirational climbing book *The Spirit of the Hills* the mountaineer F.S. Smythe devotes a whole chapter to the subject of death. He relates how once, climbing in the Alps, he fell. But what should have been a terrifying experience wasn't - such was the detachment he felt from the physical world of his body:

I was not falling, for the reason that I was not in a dimension where it was possible to fall. I, that is my consciousness, was apart from my body, and not in the least concerned with what was befalling it...

Now Smythe was a very rational man, but the experience convinced him that consciousness somehow survives death. Does it? Or does our mind just throw out some personal mental protection when our physical body is in peril? Nobody can answer that question. There are a multitude of answers.

But if our mind is just a series of electro-chemical impulses, then why do I feel as I do on the summits of mountains? Why do I pause and gaze at a truly beautiful view when I see one? Where is the benefit to a purely physical mind in the appreciation of beauty?

I don't know, I really don't, though I find there's a kind of arrogance in trying to explain such feelings away with scientific rationality. We know so little and we assume so much. Look up at the stars, the far galaxies and try to explain their creation beyond sound-bites. It's not very easy to do.

Perhaps Richard Jefferies was on the right lines when he lay on a Wiltshire hilltop besides a tumulus and realised that the concept of eternity and time passing was an illusion...

A year after my ascent of Ben Cruachan, I climbed the nearby mountain of Beinn Sgulaird from the shores of Loch Creran. The day had started overcast but by the time I was halfway up a slight breeze had swept the clouds away and I reached the summit in beautiful sunlight. Beinn Sgulaird has a broader summit than Cruachan, with ponds of water to reflect the sky and incredible views over the Highlands and the Atlantic.

Such was the loveliness of the day that I spent several hours on the summit. The clouds had gone and the breeze had died away. There was just a sky of the lightest blue reaching unbroken to the farthest Hebrides. I watched a shepherd and his dog come to the foot of the cliff below and round up his sheep. When he had gone silence returned to the mountain. A stillness and a feeling of peace.

As the sun sank in the western horizon, a great red orb against the blue and the green of the Atlantic, I felt as though the physical side of me didn't exist at all. There was no tiredness or physical struggle. Just a feeling of absolute content as though all there was of me had found a perfect sanctuary.

It was a struggle to leave it all behind and begin the descent before darkness fell over the rocky path. It was very dark before I reached the side of the loch, the mountain just a patch of darkness against the moon and the stars.

The End

John Bainbridge has a walking blog at
www.thefreedomtoroam.com
which features all the latest walks, news of access campaigns and information about the books.

John has a writing blog at
www.johnbainbridgewriter.wordpress.com

and a blog devoted to the crime novels and thrillers at
www.gaslightcrime.wordpress.com

You can order John's books directly from these blogs. Some of John's other titles are featured in the next few pages.

***THE COMPLEAT TRESPASSER** – Journeys into the heart of Forbidden Britain*
by John Bainbridge Published by Fellside Books.

In 1932, five ramblers in England were imprisoned for daring to walk in their own countryside. The Mass Trespass on to Kinder Scout, which led to their arrests, has since becoming an iconic symbol of the campaign for the freedom to roam in the British countryside.

The Compleat Trespasser – Journeys Into The Heart Of Forbidden Britain, written by outdoor journalist John Bainbridge, looks at just why the British were – and still are – denied responsible access to much of their own land. This ground-breaking book examines how events throughout history led to the countryside being the preserve of the few rather than the many.

It examines the landscapes to which access is still denied, from stretches of moorland and downland to many of our beautiful forests and woodlands. It poses the question: should we walk and trespass through these areas regardless of restrictions?

BALMORAL KILL – A Thriller by John Bainbridge

The autumn of 1937 - A desperate race against time to find a deadly killer...

In 1936 the British royal family were rocked by their greatest scandal as Edward VIII gave up the throne in order to marry an American divorcee.

Many ordinary people regretted the loss of their popular king. In the dark corridors of power, not everyone was sorry...

A year later the Abdication Crisis seems forgotten and all eyes are on the Coronation that summer. In August the new King George VI will retreat to Balmoral, his remote holiday home in the Highlands of Scotland.

As the shadow of war falls across Europe, a sinister conspiracy lies deep within the British establishment.

A man lies dead in a woodland glade. An unfortunate accident or has the first shot been fired in a secret war?

Sean Miller is recalled home to take on his deadliest challenge – but where do his loyalties really lie?

In a frantic chase, from the slums and sinister alleys of London to the lonely glens of the Scottish Highlands, Miller must hunt and bring down his most dangerous opponent.

His mission - to foil the final shot that will plunge Europe into the abyss of a new Dark Age.

LOXLEY

THE CHRONICLES
OF ROBIN HOOD

JOHN
BAINBRIDGE

1198 A.D A hooded man brings rebellion to the forest – Sherwood Forest. Lionheart's England, with the King fighting in Normandy…

For the oppressed villagers of Sherwood there is no escape from persecution and despair. They exist under the sufferance of their brutal overlords. When a mysterious stranger saves a miller's son from cruel punishment, the Sheriff of Nottingham sends the ruthless Sir Guy of Gisborne to hunt him down.

His past life destroyed, Robin of Loxley must face his greatest challenge yet. Deadly with a longbow and a sword, he will fight tyranny and injustice, encounter allies and enemies old and new. The vast Sherwood Forest with its hidden glades and ancient pathways is the last refuge of wolfsheads. Here their bloody battles will be fought, friendships forged and loyalties tested. Loxley will become Robin Hood. Notorious leader of outlaws. Their daring deeds will become legend.

Printed in Great Britain
by Amazon.co.uk, Ltd.,
Marston Gate.